"Erin teaches leaders at all levels how to discover your own authenticity, voice and personal values and then to determine whether those align with where you are right now—a true decision flow in and of itself."

— *Christopher Smurthwaite,*
Healthcare and Venture Capital Strategist

"Understanding my approach to decision making (different than problem solving) has helped me rethink the role I play. The tools in this book are very usable in real-world situations."

— *Conor Gillespie, CEO and Founder, Catalyst Companies*

"Erin challenges us to go beyond the superficial while making decisions. She seamlessly integrates methodologies to help you navigate through the burdens of decision making, looking at the individual holistically and not just in your role at the office, and provides you with options with which to experiment."

— *Regina Sherman, Executive Coach and Consultant*

"I feel better equipped to quiet all the noise and distractions that currently cause me to procrastinate making a difficult decision."

— *Michelle Standard, Healthcare Management*

"This is a worthwhile read for anyone who struggles to make decisions with confidence or bring others into a decision-making process with the right level of influence and commitment."

— *Sarah Foltz, Customer Experience Executive*

"Each chapter provides case-studies, evidence-based rationale and most importantly practical exercises which help you to learn to master the skills and habits necessary to make better and more aligned decisions."

— *Ruth Kearns, Executive Coach and Consultant*

"Written in an accessible and engaging manner, Ms. Clymer Lessard offers insightful and practical solutions to breaking through the obstacles in order to let decisions flow."

— *Sunny Lee Goodman, Executive Coach and Consultant*

The Authentic Leader's Guide
to Making the Right Decision
When the Stakes are High

DECISION
FLOW

ERIN CLYMER LESSARD

ISBN 978-1-7342979-1-1

Design by Alan Barnett

DEDICATION

*To Sylvan and Jasper for being your brilliant selves
and teaching me the importance of this work.*

TABLE OF CONTENTS

The Secret Sauce of Making Authentic Decisions

My Quarter-Century Crisis

Many years ago, I was 25 and faced with the first of many career dilemmas which felt like existential crises. I had a job that I liked and felt competent in and I was in an organization that was making a difference in ways I felt passionate about, but I had the nagging sense that I was not living up to my potential or purpose, that there was something significant I was supposed to do.

Trying to figure out what was next, I came across a Yogi Berra quote: "If you don't know where you're going, you'll end up someplace else." I panicked. I was headed to someplace else and I had no clue where it was! I was the worst decision maker! I couldn't choose a major (I'd gone through four), I couldn't decide what to do once I graduated, and although I'd landed a great job, I just wasn't satisfied.

At this point in the story, you'd expect me to share how I learned methodical decision making and developed a method that I'll share with you. Nope. That's not how it turned out. I made several more career turns over the next ten years before launching my consulting and coaching business. I've made so many big, consequential decisions with my own life (moves across the country, divorce, job changes, buying and selling houses) that I am well-versed in the mental game of weighing decisions. I call the constant stream of conflicting opinions the ticker tape that runs through our heads. I have been through a lot of ticker tape.

When I decided to leave my well-paying corporate job to launch my consultancy, I was completely naïve. I had no clue what it would take to be successful and, truth be told, if I knew then the hills and valleys that come with entrepreneurship, it might have given me pause. That would have been one of the biggest mistakes of my life! Sometimes the unlikely decision is exactly the decision we need to make.

Redo the Past? I Wouldn't Change a Thing

At a recent retreat with other coaches and consultants, we were asked to share decisions that we regretted. I was paired with a colleague to discuss, and as we mulled this question over, we came to the same conclusion—not a one. Every decision, some of them unwise, some of them unkind, many of them with the potential to be "regrettable," had led us to the very place we were as we sat across from each other on that lovely Arizona day. The decisions couldn't be seen as regrets because they had brought about too many other valuable things.

My relationship with decision making has shifted significantly since those early days of career changes and divorce. It's not that I see them as less consequential; rather, I see my role in responding to those consequences differently. For every decision, there is an outcome and a ripple effect. Many things will be impacted, some of which I can't know. It is my job to consider the downstream effects of any decision I make. It is not my job to make predictions about the future nor my responsibility to manage how others will perceive my personal decisions. I trust that, if I approach it with authenticity, I will make a sound decision with the best information in front of me. Wherever the decision leads me, I will learn, grow and thrive there.

I was once terrified that I'd end up "someplace else," as Yogi Berra warned. Now I know that we will all end up someplace unplanned and our job is to build the path as we walk it. This is what has allowed me to coach hundreds of people in ways that have radically changed their relationships with decision making.

The Importance of Getting into Decision Flow

The concept of flow was originated by Hungarian-American psychologist Mihaly Csikszentmihalyi. As he describes flow, it is the state of getting lost in one's work, where time falls aside, and one becomes completely absorbed in the task at hand. For creative flow, one must have technical knowledge in a field and the challenge level must be proportionate to the skill level.[1]

How, then, would a newly-minted leader, facing a new political environment with fresh challenges, ever find a state of decision flow? Without extensive experience in the role, how could a leader find the ease that comes with flow? Unlike Csikszentmihalyi's creative flow, where one becomes lost to oneself, decision flow requires becoming quite present and aware of oneself. It is not being lost in the work, but rather quite attuned to and aware of it.

Think of decision making like a river. Someone who makes great decisions and gets others on board is like a river, quickly and freely flowing. We all have the river. We can all be in that kind of flow. But most of us aren't. Most of us have debris—rocks, branches, eddies—that trap some of the water for a while. Sometimes those obstacles do interesting things like cause rapids or give us time to slow down and rest awhile. Sometimes they dam the whole thing up. All of those things slowing down that water serve a purpose and can be of use.

And yet, if you want to be someone whose decisions get noticed and followed, you have to be in flow. Decision flow is a state of energetic calm. Neither sleepy nor anxious, it is focused, energized presence. Decision flow is confidently facing a decision, recognizing the information you need, having easy access to contrary people and ideas that test your thinking, while having an inner sense of peace and confidence that all will be well.

To be in flow, you have to pull on your waders, get in the water, and remove the obstacles. That's what this book is designed to do—to help you identify and remove the obstacles keeping you out of decision flow.

Otto Scharmer, senior lecturer at MIT and co-founder of the Presencing Institute, said "Two leaders in the same circumstance doing the same thing can bring about completely different outcomes, depending on the inner place from which each operates."[2] A leader in flow who has removed the obstacles might come to the same conclusion as a leader who has not, but the former will get there quicker and have more success and buy-in than the latter. When we operate from a place of flow, we do so with more intuition, trust, influence, and magnetism than when we operate from a place of obstacles.

Decision making is not only about searching for more data to analyze. Information is important to make wise decisions, but alone it is more likely to leave you stuck and frustrated and entirely unlikely to get you into flow. The next three sections of this book will help you understand what flow looks like, how to find it, and how to become the person who can make decisions quickly and with buy-in.

What's in the Sauce?

Pressed to learn quickly, many professionals turn to tools to help make a decision. "Surely there's some formula I can plug all this information into and the answer will pop out!" they think. This is such a popular assumption that decision-making models are ubiquitous. Mindtools. com, an online learning platform, has an article on decision making that lists over forty tools, models, and steps for making good decisions. Forty! How is a leader ever to learn how to make good decisions when there are so many different methodologies?

The secret is this: there is no framework, application, or series of questions anyone can give you that will make decisions easier. If you're looking for a get-deciding-quick scheme, I can't help you. No one can. To be a great decision maker and someone whose decisions others want to get behind requires work. You have to become the decision maker. This book contains all the secrets that help my clients become the kind of person who can make good decisions quicker and more confidently.

Chapter One outlines the context for this book. Why the complex modern world and high-pressure work environment makes decision making so stressful and difficult. Chapter Two delves into some of my client stories so you can explore some real-world examples of the problems that leaders encounter and their journeys toward success. The "secret sauce" of this book then provides the steps that you need to take toward authentic decision making and flow. It's divided into three sections: influencing others, overcoming the obstacles to flow, and developing your inner authority.

Part One: Influencing Others

The most researched, best-intended, and the soundest decision is useless without buy-in from others. If you become the best decision maker the world has ever seen but don't learn how to bring others on board, you will be ineffective. Decisions of any consequence rarely happen in a vacuum. Even when we're deciding where to go for dinner, we often have other people with opinions on the outcome. Have you ever asked someone where they wanted to eat to have them say, "I don't care," and then when you make a suggestion, suddenly they have lots of opinions? It can be super annoying, and it's an example of the impact decisions have on others around us. Even if they say, "I'm not hungry, just make a decision and I'll drink water," they still have an opinion about ambiance.

The next two chapters will help you build your influence muscle so that your decisions have more staying power.

In Chapter Three, *Get Others on Board with Your Decisions,* we'll dive right into having conversations that change people's minds. It's a blend of advocating for what you know and building a listening muscle to understand what criteria others are prioritizing. Too often we assume that we need to get better at explaining our opinion. If we can just explain it better, we think, we'll be able to get others to buy in. Actually, it is rarely about how well you state your side, and much more often about how well you listen. When you understand what motivates others, you're better able to position your solution in a way that meets their priorities.

This chapter will also teach you how to have difficult conversations when the stakes feel high. Perhaps you've already made a decision and need to influence others to step in line. Or you're ready to draw a firm line in the sand on what you will and won't accept. This chapter will teach you the criteria for doing this successfully.

Chapter Four, *Manage Your Brain's Defensive Reactions,* focuses on the neuroscience behind our automatic reactions to threat. Our brain often gets in the way when we are trying to influence others. To effectively communicate our ideas, we need to learn to manage our protective instincts. Research tells us that we can literally shrink the amygdala, the part of our brain responsible for our emotional and stress reactions, in order to control how we deal with difficult situations.

In this chapter, you will understand why you react the way you do and learn techniques for managing your response. When you achieve this, you will be better able to get others on board with your ideas. To get people on your bus, it needs to be a smooth ride. No one wants to climb onto a bus with someone having a meltdown.

Part Two: Overcoming the Obstacles to Decision Making

This section will help you to identify and remove the barriers keeping you from being someone who makes decisions others want to follow. You can research every tool available on decision making, but if you don't master the work in these next three chapters, you will never be in decision flow. This is the gooey inside section. Think of it as a truffle: soft, mushy, maybe a little bitter in places, but sweet overall. These are the most important chapters of this book. They might be the most uncomfortable too. Those who dive in will find their flow.

In Chapter Five, *Reinvent Your Role and Expectations,* we'll explore your assumptions, the roles you take on and how they become obstacles. Roles as straightforward as "problem solver" get in our way, even if they make us successful in our jobs. To understand this obstacle, you'll outline all the roles you assume, what meaning you make of them, and how they might serve as obstacles. As you begin to redefine your roles, you'll start to feel flow.

This chapter pairs well with the *Influencing* section of the book. As you start to redefine your roles, you will likely need to have some "real talk" with others who have a stake in your staying just the way you are. Employees, for example, may not like it if you stop solving their problems (see the client example in Chapter Two), but it will be required for you to be in flow.

Chapter Six, *Stop the Back-and-Forth*, tackles the mental ticker tape we all experience when faced with a complex decision. "Part of me thinks this, but part of me thinks that…" This doesn't mean you're schizophrenic; it means you're normal. Being able to recognize and separate those different opinions, however, is critical to finding flow.

Sometimes the ticker tape brings us the inner critic—a lovely little voice who wants to make sure we don't get in over our head. While some suggest you can simply brush the critic away, that is rarely successful. Instead, you will learn what the critic is concerned with and how to negotiate with it.

Chapter Seven, *Get Over the Stories of Past Failure*, will bring you face-to-face with the negative memories that you hold on to. The stories that have you thinking you're no good at making decisions. Most of us have failures in our past. Some of us wear them like an albatross hung around our neck as a reminder. Shame is a dam in your river and will slow down any movement toward flow. When you hold on to those old stories, you will be stuck.

This chapter will give you the power to retell your stories and reclaim your victories. Failure is only a bad word if you don't learn from it.

Part Three: Developing Your Inner Authority

The final section focuses on who you are and what matters to you. When you've learned to have the right conversations, and you've removed the obstacles in the way of your flow, you're ready to find your inner decision maker.

Chapter Eight, *Discover Your Values and Your Authentic Voice,* is one of the most tactical in this book. It is centered around knowing the values that determine what matters to you and how they influence your decisions. This chapter contains a process for uncovering your unique values and understanding how to use them to make authentic decisions.

Chapter Nine, *Does Your Company Deserve You?,* is your "come-to-Jesus" moment. Sometimes, no matter how good you get at influencing, finding decision flow, and speaking from inner authority, your organization is just not the right fit for you. If you're unsure that any of this work will help you succeed in your company, it might be them, not you. Not every person is a natural fit in every company. Even the most developed, advanced professionals sometimes land in companies with cultures that clash. This isn't anyone's failure, but it does require some action.

This chapter will help you to assess if it's you or them and what to do if you discover it's them.

The final chapters of the book, *How to Stay on Track* and *What to Do Now*, help you to create a "what's next" plan and offer my parting thoughts on why all of this work matters so much for my clients and their organizations.

The chapters in this book are intended to build upon each other, but reading them out of order won't make them ineffective. Most of this book can be read in any order, except for Chapter Eight. You will get the most out of the values if you first work through the chapters in the *Obstacles* section. Without that under your belt, your values might be a little thin and have less meaning for you.

These chapters share the method behind my work with hundreds of clients. I give them to you with the hope that you can find flow and start to make authentic decisions.

CHAPTER 1

Why is Decision Making so Difficult?

Losing Your Decision-Making Mojo

My client, John, had achieved his company's top performance award by the time he was 27. His customer service scores exceeded his peers' month after month. The CEO knew his name. When he was quickly promoted to head a customer service department, peers and executives alike congratulated him and wished him well for this hard-earned recognition.

A month into the job, now responsible for a critical project intended to boost the company's customer service scores, he wasn't sure what he'd gotten himself into. The team member he appointed to lead the initiative was missing key deadlines. John's boss was holding his feet to the fire, demanding updates and being explicit about his disappointment. He was putting in longer hours than ever before trying to solve the problem and he was bewildered by how he had ended up in this position. Just a month ago, he knew exactly how to solve the problems that came his way. Now he was floundering.

I see this again and again in my clients, from first-time leaders to new division heads: the rewarding promotion becomes the thing that grinds them to a halt and leaves them with a confused sense of their success and ability. Where they were once masterful decision makers, they now feel incompetent. So, why does this keep happening? What is the common thread?

Decision Making or Problem Solving?

If you are a leader, chances are that you have gotten to where you are, in part, because you're a great problem solver. Business loves problem solvers. They work out sticky situations seemingly with ease. They un-stick stalled processes. They teach others how to resolve things. They turn our messes into something simpler that seems so obvious in retrospect. They take care of things so others don't have to. What a wonderful skill to possess! No wonder it propels you toward recognition and success.

Like John, I see many leaders promoted based on their problem-solving skills, who then suddenly find themselves no longer able to solve the challenges in front of them. The problems become more complex and require a new level of information sharing and buy-in. The well-worn tools, that they are masterful at wielding, no longer work. They don't know how to decide the right course of action. The problem confounds them.

This is often because they are confusing problem solving and decision making.

Problem solving is removing a roadblock, correcting a wrong turn, recovering something that has gone amuck. It requires something to be wrong; it requires a problem. It is, by nature, an investigation and analysis of something that has already occurred.

Decision making, on the other hand, is about setting a course for the future. It requires a question: How can we reach that goal? Which strategy do we choose? Which job should I choose? Am I ready to commit to that? Sometimes, a problem solver must investigate what caused the need for change but a decision maker always chooses what to do next.

Decision making is forward-thinking, setting a future course, where problem solving is backward-looking, analyzing what went wrong and course-correcting.

When problems are simple, like why we missed that deadline, the distinction between decision making and problem solving is smaller. We missed the deadline because Anthony became a bottleneck; to resolve it, we'll distribute tasks more evenly among the team. There is a forward-looking solution (a decision to be made) but it's a straightforward derivative of the problem.

When problems are complex, like why we missed our goals this month, problem solvers yield simplistic solutions where decision makers take bold steps. A problem solver will focus on what went wrong with the goals. For example, "We have a declining conversion rate, so let's increase our call volume." A decision maker will see complex factors and choose a new course: "We have a declining conversion rate with our current strategy, so let's employ inbound marketing and measure the impact." The problem solver finds a fix (increasing call volume) to the problem of conversion rates, but is focused on a simple solution. In choosing a new strategy, the decision maker creates something original that addresses the problem in a bolder way.

When leaders confuse the two, they may waste time investigating problems rather than generating new ideas and answers. A problem solver focuses on the minutia. A decision maker sees the big picture. Leaders transitioning to larger roles are faced with a larger scope of influence where this understanding of the big picture is essential. While attracted to the prestige of the new role, few consider this required shift in perspective and style.

Decision Fatigue and the Illusion of Control

We are built to desire control and authority over our lives. A 2016 study[3] on people's desire for power identified two kinds: an interest in influence over others ("power over") and an interest in autonomy ("power within"). While people often refer to power as "being in charge" and climbing the corporate constructs, the study participants revealed that autonomy is much more attractive. When asked to choose between having authority over others or having autonomy, nearly two-thirds opted for autonomy. We want to be able to make our own choices.

High performers who are not yet managers often confuse the two. They think, "When I'm in charge and can make the decisions, this place will run so much more smoothly." They envision a world where their decision-making skills are superior. Yet everyone who has advanced through an organization knows that when they are actually in the decision-making seat they must contend with the expectations of management above and the employees below whose futures are in their hands. The pressure builds and the dream of quick-and-easy decision making fades. While they may have gained influence and power over their direct reports ("power over"), they have lost autonomy ("power within") because of the greater number of people relying on them.

This can be a difficult transition. At this level, decision making has as much to do with influencing and communicating with peers and managers as it does choosing between alternatives. Finding the best path requires an honest analysis of what is likely to get buy-in from above and below. Decisions might have seemed black and white in an autonomous world, but now they are grey, foggy, and complicated. Your success depends on whether others feel you've made the right decision.

While some decisions are drawn-out, high-stakes affairs, most leaders make lots of smaller decisions constantly throughout the day. People knock on your door, send another email, stop you in the hall, announce it in a meeting, and you are expected to provide the solution. You're in charge, you're their chief problem solver, and they don't have a lot of time for you to mull it over. They need your decision fast.

Many of my clients stand on the thin precipice of decision overwhelm. On one side sits the thrill and adrenaline of getting it right. When they are in flow, making good calls, and solving people's problems, it's like a drug; once they've experienced it, they crave more of it. On the other side of this precipice sits exhaustion and foggy thinking. When there are so many emails, each of them needing thought and an answer, the gears gum up. The system gets overheated and decision-making functions shut down. They start to procrastinate and second-guess and ask for more time. They know there can be a flow to decision making, that it doesn't have to be so hard, that it can even feel good. But it's so far from their current state that the very knowledge that the flow state exists pushes them further into the fog.

Roy Baumeister and Jean Twenge call this "decision fatigue." Their research at Case Western Reserve

University[4] suggests that the pressure of decision making reduces willpower and self-control. Rooted in the psychological notion of ego depletion, the researchers discovered that we become mentally exhausted from the repeated demand to make decisions—even banal ones like what clothes to wear or what to make for dinner. The sheer volume of decisions drains our limited pool of mental resources, impacting our ability to make future decisions.

If you've ever worked through an email inbox with tens, if not hundreds, of messages and felt overwhelmed, you've experienced decision fatigue. The act of responding to email after email, making recommendations and decisions with each returned message, can cause mental exhaustion that leads to sloppy decisions. As willpower and self-control diminish, each answer becomes less thoughtful. Every hour, someone in a cubicle rolls their eyes and says, "They clearly didn't read the email." Leaders are responding quickly and missing key information because they are overloaded with small decisions.

Making Time for the Important, Not Just the Urgent

Almost every one of my clients struggles with time and prioritization. As companies seek to become more efficient, they often ask leaders to do more work with fewer resources, leaving people with overrun email inboxes and an unrelenting meeting schedule. Everything feels urgent and they strive to swiftly work against the clock. Often the urgent gets in the way of the important. When leaders strive to solve problems quickly, all day long, they fail to carve out time for the important decisions that cannot be made quickly. Restructures, strategic shifts, relationships with colleagues in other divisions, and development conversations with team members all get pushed off the agenda when the next urgent email comes in.

They aren't doing it to be neglectful. The fires *are* often fires. But careers don't progress when they ignore their boss's emails and "management" is often a huge culprit of the email deluge. Feeling the pressure coming in from all sides, leaders tackle the easiest things first, putting out the fires they know they can quash.

The problem is that, when they don't take the time for important decisions, nothing changes and the pressure they feel won't relent. As long as they are in a constant reactive state, they will not change the dynamic, and they will miss the important things. Remember, it is the important decisions that have the biggest impact on your decision-making reputation. Even if you are the best firefighter, if you aren't getting to the important decisions, you will not be seen as someone capable of leading at the next level.

This book will help you learn how to become the type of person who can focus on the important, not just the urgent.

The Influence of Corporate Politics on Decision Making

Corporate politics add another layer to the complexity of decision making. Leaders in the middle of organizations are in a vice between competing stakeholders. They feel loyal to and protective of the people they manage and are responsible for and desire the attention of management above them. They often describe this to me as "serving two masters."

In his book, *The Five Dysfunctions of a Team*[5], Patrick Lencioni talks about "first teams." This is the expectation that a leader is first a member of the team they sit on—consisting of their peers and their boss—and that their loyalties belong here. This means that the agenda and strategy of the organization trumps a leader's protection of the people below them, which is an incredibly hard lesson for most new leaders. Some never learn it, and it stops their career progression.

The phrase "corporate politics" doesn't have to be shudder-inducing. Here's how I define politics with my clients: the art of knowing the culture, values, and expectations of your management, peers, and those with influence, and behaving with that knowledge in mind. It doesn't have to mean manipulation and doublespeak, the characteristics sometimes given to "corporate politics." It does mean listening to what is important to other people and making strategic choices informed by that information.

Leaders in the middle of organizations must learn this influencing skill to continue advancing. And it complicates decision making. It is not enough to make the best decision. A leader must also make the best decision that resonates with management.

Managing and Influencing Are Different Skills

The number one challenge that every leader assuming a new role must overcome is learning that what made them successful before will not make them successful now. With every promotion, decision making changes and successful leaders need to learn the new rules.

My client Claire was in a new leadership role and had not yet learned the power of influence (rather than directing) to get her team to rise to new challenges. She'd been an effective project manager, leading multimillion-dollar projects to successful completion within time and budget. She was used to being in charge, directive and on point. When she was promoted to an oversight role, her relationships with the staff changed. She realized that trust was low when her employees brought their complaints about each other to her. Now at the center, she saw how their infighting was diminishing productivity. Her one-on-one conversations were not changing the team dynamic and she began to doubt her ability to improve the inner workings of the team. Her boss commented on the team's "vibe." What used to feel like easy decision making now had more visibility, higher expectations, and unfamiliar components. So, she returned to her comfort zone and began to micromanage. She put in more hours, looked for more information to analyze, and spent more time making the kind of decisions she was comfortable with but that her staff should have been making.

She came to one of our sessions burnt-out and recognizing something needed to change. Her staff were not stepping up to take back their responsibilities. Their team dynamic was getting no better. The runway she had been promised from upper management was running out and she wasn't creating the turnaround she had guaranteed them.

She was in an unsustainable pattern borne of clinging to what was familiar—what she knew she could be successful at—rather than learning the type of decision-making skills required to be successful at her new role and level in the organization. Claire and I worked together to help her build relationships and develop people to make their own decisions and solve their own problems. I taught her how to show management she was asking the right questions of her team, not micromanaging the budget the same way she had done as a project manager.

The Complexities of Collaborative Decision Making

Much has been made about the volatile, uncertain, complex, and ambiguous (VUCA) world that corporations now function in. Every business journal has written about the challenges the current global environment poses for business. Leaders are not making simple decisions with autonomy. They are making complex decisions, with multiple factors to consider, that impact the rest of the organization. This reality has given rise to the matrixed organization. Where there was once a linear hierarchy of command and control, the matrixed organization recognizes that decisions don't influence silos alone; one division's choice to outsource will impact another division's union contract. Individuals don't just report up a chain of command, they now report sideways and diagonally to ensure comprehensive decision making. While important and useful, these structures come with unique challenges. Leaders rarely have the autonomy to make decisions about matters that directly impact their team.

This dilemma became evident in a project I ran with a team of leaders in a large multinational company. The division comprised many different products and services. Naturally, it was quite siloed. To combat this, the division created a culture where buy-in was an expectation before decisions became finalized. A team leader could not decide in isolation. Instead, they had to speak with leaders of other teams and management, sometimes for even simple decisions. The leaders complained of having no clear decision rights. They had no clarity on when they were empowered to make a decision. To protect themselves and their teams, they erred on the side of not making decisions until every possible stakeholder had been consulted. Often, they left it up to leaders above them to make the final call. The outliers who pushed ahead without "enough" consultation were reprimanded and branded as "working against the culture."

This division is not unique. *Forbes, Harvard Business Review,* and *The Economist* have all written about the negative impact of collaboration. Though well-intended, generous collaborators often become called on to offer input on projects outside of their scope of expertise. As they advance in the organization, they produce bottlenecks, slowing the speed of decisions. Collaborative and complex decision making has become the norm and it is creating a cohort of leaders who have lost their ability to trust their intuition, seek the right level of input and make important decisions quickly.

If you identify with this dilemma, you must feel like you're experiencing the perfect storm. If you feel that the higher you get in an organization, the harder it becomes to make decisions, you are right. Many leaders fear they've lost their ability to make decisions altogether.

Remember John at the beginning of this chapter? Six months into the new role, the pressure was mounting on all sides. He came home from his stressful job to a stressful home life, not because someone wasn't doing what he thought they would do, but because life with children is always disorderly and unpredictable. It requires patience, restraint, and presence. At the end of a day full of overturned tables at work, those qualities were hard to come by.

One morning, John stood in front of the mirror, wound so tight he could not see a way forward. Something needed to give. He grabbed a razor, stood in front of his bathroom mirror, and cut off the beard that had been his signature look for ten years. He needed a dramatic change in his mental model and wanted a symbol to remind him. He also wanted everyone to see that things were different. His world was in such chaos that he felt his only way forward was a drastic measure. Predictably, he shocked people when he returned to work the next day.

While not always so dramatic, most high-performing professionals can relate to the feeling of pressure coming from all sides. A feeling of being trapped that is unending and impossible. John's story is extreme, but it's far from unique. Every day I work with clients struggling to manage the expectations of their jobs.

Leaders must relearn a few things to return to being the successful, confident and influential decision makers they once were.

What Kind of Decision Maker are You?

To find your decision-making mojo in your current environment, it's helpful to begin by getting clear on what kind of decision maker you are now. I like to call these decision-making archetypes.

An archetype is a personality or behavior, often used to categorize people. If you think of popular psychological models, you'll recognize different archetypes. Type A and B are archetypes. Introvert/extrovert are archetypes. We all fall into some patterns when it comes to decision making, and it's helpful to give them a descriptive archetype so you can identify your starting point.

What patterns do you notice about your decision making? Do you find yourself repeating phrases? How would others describe you?

Here are a few archetypes I've seen. Maybe one of these fits you well and you can adapt it. Better yet, create a new one that is specifically yours:

- Excited puppy: Going after decisions with gusto and full commitment until someone throws in a new toy, then becoming distracted and pursuing something else with gusto.

- Father knows best: Making decisions independently and expecting everyone to get in line without taking on board their opinions.

- Brooding teen: Being a victim of others' rules and bemoaning their lack of independence and authority.
- Careful engineer: Stress-testing everything and wanting a lot of input to ensure all information has been weighed and assessed.

You might find that you have two archetypes: one for home and one for work. Play around with this. Don't worry about finding absolute answers. The goal of this exercise is to uncover some truth about how you make decisions, not to perfectly analyze your decision-making history.

Being a respected decision maker in a complex environment is a skill that lands my clients their promotions, dream jobs, and the confidence to excel. This book lays out the secrets to move from an unclear path to the archetype of the authentic leader. First, we need to understand what authenticity looks like.

CHAPTER 2

Stories of Transformed Decision Makers

I've spent a decade as an executive coach, helping leaders find their decision flow. I spent the decade before that in the trenches of leadership, in companies large and small, in nonprofit and corporate environments. I share the stories below so you can see what is possible when a leader chooses to grow and commits to finding their authentic decision flow. As in the rest of this book, I've changed the names, industries and minor details of the client stories to protect confidentiality. However, in every story, the struggle and the outcomes are real.

Tanya:
Learning to Make
Decisions with Others

Tanya was steely when we first started working together. She was a tough go-getter and esteemed by management. They saw big things for her, but knew she had to smooth out some sharp edges to be successful. She saw herself against the world. She had overcome many obstacles in her life and that steeliness had served her survival. She was a confident decision maker but was losing the support of others around her. When team members approached her with questions, she was short and dismissive, so they avoided her as best they could. In meetings, she defended her opinions with a raised voice and, when others disagreed, she sat back with arms crossed and a scowl on her face.

Her team resented her authoritarian air. Her peers didn't trust her. Management thought she had potential but wouldn't promote her if she couldn't learn to bring others on board. As we worked together, Tanya accepted the impact her demeanor was having on her success. Without others in her corner, she was meeting resistance and struggling to bring about the changes she knew would benefit the organization. She learned to bring others into the decision-making process by listening as much as she talked. She practiced by inviting others to solve the problems they presented to her. She learned to guide their decision making instead of doubling down on her opinions. As she did this, she built a connection with her team and their performance skyrocketed. Together, they were able to implement several new processes that improved their efficiency and reduced their budget.

Tanya shifted her perspective from defending her opinions and being frustrated when others dug in their heels, to engaging others in decision making, which allowed for improved performance and quicker adoption.

Anders: Defending Bad Behaviors isn't Authenticity

Anders was a fun and engaging leader with energy that filled a room. His laughter could be heard throughout the floor and his bold personality attracted people to him. Confident in his style, both in dress and leadership, he was quick to challenge anyone who gave him feedback. "Let me stop you right there," he would say, "You don't have to like my style, but you have to respect who I am and how I do my business."

Anders was often abrasive. He believed in "telling it like it is" and was quick to let both his peers and his manager know it. He believed he was living authentically by defending his instincts. He was charismatic enough that people let him get away with it.

We started working together when Anders' manager became concerned that he was jeopardizing his and the department's reputation. Anders' team had challenging goals and would need partnership from other departments to achieve them. His charm was not making up for his sharp tongue and he was burning bridges with the people he needed to influence.

As Anders identified his true values, not those he'd adopted to protect himself from criticism, he began to see that he was defending against perceived threats. When he set aside his "tell it like it is" persona and instead leveraged his value of connection, he was able to mend these bridges and get others on board. Rather than using "authenticity" as a battering ram, he began to lead with trust and support and discovered that he garnered more respect and people started coming to him for counsel. As he turned his behavior around, he was able to lead his team to exceed the stretch goals set for them.

Gayle:
Problem-Solver-in-Chief Can't
Solve the Right Problems

Gayle thought her biggest leadership quality was solving other people's problems. She had a generous heart and people often came to her for advice. She found it easier to solve the problem for them, than to take the time to coach them to a decision. Her days were full of people coming to her—many not even in her department—so she could fix their issues. She was popular and her team and peers adored her.

But Gayle's boss was frustrated that she was putting off tough decisions that the business needed her to make. She had budget overruns and underperforming staff and the organization's leaders were losing faith in her ability to lead the department.

Gayle had to learn to develop her team and go through the uncomfortable growing pains (her and her team's) of coaching them to find a solution rather than solving it for them. She had to become a tougher boss and peer with elevated expectations of what other people were capable of. As she established this, two things happened. First, her team started rising to the challenge and solving problems without coming to Gayle. As they got better, they got quicker and their performance issues turned around. Second, as her team became more adept at making decisions and bringing fewer problems to her, she had more time to tackle the bigger decisions that needed to be made.

She had confused decision making with problem solving and assumed that, as long as she was solving issues, she'd be seen as a confident decision maker. But she was avoiding the important decisions that required more time and had bigger consequences. When management saw her direct her attention to the important issues and observed that she didn't lose the support of her team, even when implementing unpopular decisions, they awarded her the top performance award. She's now on course for a promotion.

Angela:
Discovering What's
Important in Career Decisions

Angela had a successful executive career. She'd led a large multinational division and had been at the helm of turning around an underperforming team. She was tired and knew that the division needed a different leader to lead the next leg of their journey. But she was unclear on what she wanted to do next and even how to go about deciding.

She was passionate about the organization's work and hesitant to leave it. Most executives would announce retirement but Angela wasn't willing to accept that she needed to leave the company to fulfill her purpose.

Instead of cutting ties, she examined what was important to her and discovered that there were several special projects where she knew she would make a meaningful contribution. She approached the CEO about a change in focus and stepped down from a highly visible role with a lot of prestige to a behind-the-scenes position crafted to meet both the company's needs and her passions. This change required significant character. Many executives leave because they don't know how to manage a perceived status drop, but Angela learned to manage her defensive reactions. Angela's efforts to understand who she was and what was important to her, enabled her to hold her head high, unencumbered by loss of status. She knew that her decision was right for her and nothing to feel shame in. A year later, she was sleeping better, spending more time with her family, and feeling a stronger sense of commitment to her company. She knew she was creating the impact she wanted to.

Derek:
Redefining Success
to Make the Tough Calls

Derek believed he had to succeed, no matter what. Having grown up in poverty, he worked his way into a high-profile executive role for a large company. Each success had launched him into the next opportunity. It also caused him fear that he was just one failure away from collapse. "Only winning" he'd tell his team, like a coach giving a pep talk at halftime. As the stakes got higher in each progressive role, the fear of failure grew.

He began putting off decisions. He'd claim he needed more information. He'd blame other departments for dragging their feet and trying to sabotage his team. Everywhere he looked, he saw the cliff of failure and he scrambled to stay away from the edge, which meant staying away from tough decisions.

As I coached Derek, we challenged the definitions of success and failure. We faced the fear of collapse head-on and redefined that too. Armed with the knowledge that fear was preventing him from the very success he craved, Derek was able to find small experiments that tested his limits. He stopped talking about what others weren't doing and instead talked about what he hadn't done. This accountability inspired his team toward higher engagement levels. They brought more ideas forward and he got better at listening to them.

He started testing decisions with stakeholders and when he received negative feedback, he reframed the outcome. Rather than perceiving it as a "failure" he valued this new information that would lead toward a better decision.

In each of these stories, you'll notice that my clients didn't need different decision-making tools or processes. They needed to understand what was influencing their ability to make good decisions, why others had the perceptions they did of their decisions, and how to decide from a place of confidence and inner authority that doesn't shut others out but invites them in.

They needed to recognize gaps between the intent of their actions and the impact it was having on others.

PART 1

INFLUENCING OTHERS

CHAPTER 3

Get Others on Board with Your Decisions

Why Won't People Just Do What You Suggest?

What do conversations and listening have to do with decision making? Everything. We rarely make any kind of decision, of any consequence, in a vacuum. Even seemingly mundane decisions require the buy-in of other people. Let me give you the perfect example, disguised as a fight my husband and I had the other night over a new reward system for our five- and three-year-olds.

We needed to put a hard stop on some annoying behavior that had found a foothold in our family life and were ready to try positive reinforcement for good behavior. Enter the star chart. I think it's a rite of passage for parents. Children delight in getting to put a sticker on a piece of paper. You would think that creating a chart for stickers would be simple. However, a heated debate ensued on how best to implement this system: should it just be a reward for using their cool-down spaces? Could it also be a system for implementing simple chores like picking up toys? Were we making it too complicated? Let's make the chart a picture they have to fill in to get a treat—no, not like that, like this. What are you thinking? That will never work. You're going to confuse them. You aren't making this rewarding enough for them—you're taking all the fun out of it. They're going to think they get a star for everything that we expect them to do anyway.

Blood pressure was up, frustration was high, and we were not speaking kindly to each other. Over a star chart.

Except this wasn't really about a star chart at all. While we were literally arguing about how many stars it would take to fill in a picture of an ice cream cone, we were actually arguing about how to raise boys that are respectful and create a peaceful home. The stakes were not high over the chart, but the stakes were very high in terms of the big picture.

In our desire to get it right, we were each focused on small details, unable to recognize our shared goal. Whether or not the chart was shaped like a treat would have little impact on the success of the program we were implementing. We were trying to solve it individually, not collectively, and because the stakes were high, we dug in our heels.

When we see ourselves as the sole entity responsible for a high-stakes decision, we set ourselves up for failure. We must bring others in early, and often, because the stakes are high for them as well.

In our work settings, arguments arise. Like the star chart example, they can be over seemingly unimportant details, but they often relate to much broader, complex and underlying concerns that you have to recognize before you are able to agree on a way forward. Sometimes they are confrontational. Though they can be uncomfortable, debates are productive because opinions get shared and differences aired, if not resolved immediately. Far more common and much less helpful are the arguments that take the form of silent dismissal and stealth counter-actions. It often happens that someone "agrees," or at least doesn't publicly dissent, to a decision but then takes measures independently that work against the decision they just agreed to. For example, consider a scenario where new customer relationship management (CRM) software is implemented. It's rolled out, everyone is trained, and expectations of how to use it are clear. Heads nod and people go on their way. Some will adapt their practices immediately, finding it a little clunky but taking the time to get the new system right. Others will continue to use their old Excel spreadsheets to track their customer engagements. Maybe they'll say that they're too busy now and will convert it all later, but they probably will not follow through unless their feet are put to the fire. No argument ensues, but the silent veto derails the success of the new CRM, without the opportunity to discuss why there was disagreement in the first place.

Even when your decision is a great one, if it does not get the buy-in necessary to ensure strong implementation, it will not be viewed as a good decision. Your effectiveness relies in part on your ability to make the right decision, and in part on your ability to convince others of it.

We need to understand the argument we are really having. For the CRM implementation, is the argument about the time and work required to switch to a new system? Or is it about challenging somebody's tried-and-true method? Resistance to change is rarely about the decision (though that is what people will talk about) and it is almost always about the cost to individuals to make the change.

To influence others and have the right conversations, you must learn four critical skills:

- Finding shared goals
- Questioning your assumptions
- Learning to listen, and
- Bringing it back to the subject at hand.

Finding Shared Goals

The star chart argument wasn't about the star chart at all; it was an expression of our fear and anxiety about being able to change an unacceptable pattern in our household. At no point did we pull ourselves up out of the weeds to remember why we were creating this miserable chart. Instead, we expressed our fear by trying to control the one thing we knew we had some influence over—the creation of a reward chart.

In their book, *Crucial Conversations*[6], Grenny, Patterson, Switzler, and McMillan highlight the importance of finding common goals in a disagreement. When both parties feel like they are at loggerheads and an agreed-upon solution is impossible, finding a shared goal is the first step to moving forward.

In the CRM software example, the leader needs to come back to the shared goal, explaining the "why" for the change. The resistant salesperson needs to be engaged in a conversation about the intent and what's in it for him or her. A conversation might sound like this:

"I know this change is asking a lot of you. You have a system that's worked for you for years. I'm asking you to invest time in learning to do it a new way when it's likely to be less accurate while you're getting used to it. Here's why this switch matters to us as a company and to you as a sales manager: we have done a miserable job of cross-selling because we don't share information about our customers. You keep information about key accounts that other divisions would benefit from. When we sell in silos, it annoys the customer. We even try to sell them things they are already using because we don't know someone has already had that conversation. This CRM change will enable you to have better customer service and improve your customer satisfaction scores. It's not just about you sharing your information, but it's also others sharing their information with you. When your scores go up, your bonus goes up. This system will help us all provide better service, the company will increase its revenue and we'll all benefit from that."

If your implementation conversations stop at training, you will not win the hearts and minds of people who are impacted by your decisions. You will not get buy-in if you cannot communicate the shared goals.

To find shared goals, you have to understand the fears, assumptions, and expectations of others.

Questioning Your Assumptions

We evolved to make snap decisions. We jump to conclusions to speed up our processing time; our brains make assumptions based on past data. This works to our advantage in many instances. Historically, it helped us determine friend or foe quickly to protect our community. In the modern day, it improves our cognitive reasoning in many ways, including how quickly we can process words when reading. We use contextual clues and make assumptions about the words we read on a page—we don't sound out every letter. Facebook is full of memes suggesting you're special if you can read a paragraph with missing letters but, in actuality, most readers make the cognitive leap because their brain fills in the gaps. This quick processing simplifies our cognitive computing so we can save our energy for the tougher problems.

While jumping to conclusions can save us time and effort, it is not always the case.

As you read this next story, I want you to underline what is factual. Test yourself for anything that has interpretation or nuance in it. I want you to only identify that which is truly a fact.

At the end of a conference call, I was trying to arrange a follow-up meeting with several hard-to-schedule colleagues. It looked like there was no time, so someone suggested 7 a.m. I knew my colleague Emily had to do pre-school drop-off and couldn't make that time and, wanting to help promote a mom-friendly culture, I mentioned that to the group and suggested we keep working to find a time that Emily could join. Emily was often hard to work with and another colleague told me Emily was jealous of me, so I was trying to make an effort to build rapport. Afterward, Emily came up to me smugly and said, "I know you're new to corporate, so you probably don't know this, but it was inappropriate to call me out as not being able to make that time. As a working mom, I don't want others to think I can't do things. Be more aware next time." The gall! I was helping her! Next time I'm looking out for myself and she can deal with whatever the outcome!

How much of that story was fact? Very little. Most of it is assumption, interpretation, and nuance. Here are the facts:

- There was a conference call; it ended.
- A meeting needed to be scheduled.
- The storyteller finds Emily hard to work with (that she is hard to work with is not a fact.)
- Emily spoke to the storyteller after the call.

Here are the interpreted parts of the story that many people assume are fact and why they are, actually, not fact:

- The colleagues are hard to schedule. It might be true that, in that moment, no one was sharing times that overlapped, but in many corporate environments, when something is deemed important, people will rearrange schedules and find the time. It is not necessarily a fact that this group is hard to schedule.
- Emily had to drop her kids off at preschool. Again, this is assumed based on prior conversations or past information. The storyteller does not know whether Emily could ask someone else to do drop-off. She assumes that there is only one possible scenario.
- Emily is hard to work with. The storyteller experiences that, but it is not a fact.
- Emily is jealous. This is hearsay and not fact.

The storyteller's actions were coming from a good place. She was trying to build rapport with a new colleague and promote a culture of inclusivity. Our assumptions are not always tainted with malintent. They are usually well-intended but that doesn't mean they are any less problematic.

Before getting frustrated by another's actions or reactions, it's helpful to consider how we move quickly from data to assumption and action and how this can skew decision making.

First, we have a pool of information and data. All of the facts of a story. As evidenced above, not every story is pure fact. From that data, we select information to pay attention to. We don't have time to process every bit of information, so we choose what seems pertinent. Here is the first opportunity for bias and error. Next, from the evidence we choose to pay attention to, we interpret what it means. Once we've interpreted it, we draw some assumptions and conclusions that we make meaning out of and, finally, we choose an action.[7]

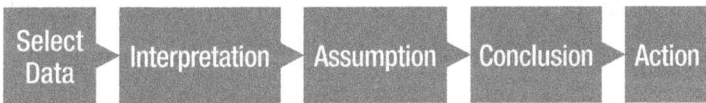

Select Data	Interpretation	Assumption	Conclusion	Action

In the conference call story, the storyteller chose data that her colleague had to do drop-off on a particular day. She then interpreted this data as something that had to happen every day, without exception. She assumed that Emily couldn't make an early meeting and also that Emily would appreciate her standing up for that "fact." She concluded that she needed to advocate for Emily and acted on that belief by stating it on the call.

You can also carry this forward by examining the storyteller's likely future actions. She has now drawn a firmer conclusion about Emily being hard to work with and has decided that she must look out for herself. She's forming beliefs about Emily's character that will influence how she acts around her in the future.

In this scenario, it's clear to see the impact assumptions can have on our interactions with others. Each assumption, carried out to a conclusion and action, informs the data we select to interpret in the next interaction.

It is also important to recognize the impact this has on our ability to influence others. We have to acknowledge that our interpretation of others is often based on our own assumptions and conclusions, rather than their reality. When this mismatch guides our actions, the other person may feel like they are not being understood and will be less likely to connect with you or get on board with your decisions. To explore this, it is helpful to work through the data-to-action process with a particular situation you are facing, examining alternative interpretations along the way.

Exercise: Challenge Your Assumptions

Consider a decision you have recently implemented, or are about to implement, and identify an individual who has disagreed—either publicly and verbally, or silently by working around you. Using the data-to-action process, identify what interpretations, assumptions, and conclusions have driven you to your actions involving that individual. What might you need to reconsider?

Now, apply the same process to the individual. Imagine what interpretations, assumptions, and conclusions might be leading to her or his actions. (Note: this is an entirely speculative exercise and should be used to build empathy, not solidify new beliefs about other people.) How could this exploration help you understand what matters to this individual so you can identify a shared goal?

Learning to Listen

Listening is an under-utilized skill, primarily because we're often stuck in problem-solving mode. When we listen with the intent of solving a problem, we often miss what someone is saying and instead focus on what we think about what they are saying.

You can assess your listening skills with a simple test. The next time someone is talking to you, what questions do you ask? Are they fact-gathering questions to help you make sense of the story or problem? Or do your questions focus on how the other person feels about the story they are sharing? I would put money on your answer being the former. Because we are often rewarded for problem solving and offering insight, it requires great restraint to actively shut that function off and just become curious about the person talking. This is at the heart of good listening and it is a learned skill for most of us.

The problem with problem solving is that we listen to the wrong things. When we listen for facts, we jump to conclusions about what they mean, and we miss the information about feelings, values and meaning that others are sharing.

In *Creating Intelligent Teams,* by Anne Rod and Marita Fridjhon, the authors outline three levels of listening in teams. They are profoundly different and impact your ability to get buy-in:

- **Level 1: Internal Listening.** It is all about me, myself and I. I will associate freely and let my opinion be known and I may interrupt others to do so.

- **Level 2: Focused Listening.** I listen with the intent to understand what the others are saying. I can build upon their comments, either through deepening questions or other further reflections.

- **Level 3: Global Listening.** I listen to what is not being said; what is wanting to be said but not expressed; what is between the lines of the words already spoken; and what is in the atmosphere of the team.

When we focus on Levels 2 and 3, we can connect with others in a way that deepens our understanding and helps others feel heard. Most people cannot buy into a change until they feel heard by someone. If you want your decisions to have a successful implementation, you need to learn to make others feel heard.

If you are reading this and think you've got this covered, please take a deeper look. I've worked with plenty of people who functioned at Level 1 and thought they were at Level 2. If you can build on others' ideas, yet you listen primarily with the intent to find the next thing to say, it is still all about you. If, while you listen to others speak, you are thinking of a response or retort, you are listening at Level 1.

Level 2 is about the other person, not about you. At Level 2 you remain open and curious while the other person is speaking. If a question forms, it is a clarifying question, borne out of curiosity about their experience. Level 2 listening is slower than most corporate environments allow.

I worked with an executive team that claimed to be Level 2 listeners. Some of them even claimed to be Level 3. And while they often remained quiet and listened for what was unspoken, they were doing so with an eye toward political safety. Their "reading between the lines" was a protective reaction, searching for signals that the space wasn't safe, and their silence was due to fear of speaking up.

Bringing It Back to the Subject at Hand

When people are confronted with something uncomfortable, like not meeting expectations, or actively working against a new process that's being implemented, they often muddy the waters by bringing distractions into the conversation. If a leader confronts a sales manager about not adopting the new CRM system, for example, the sales manager could divert the conversation to discuss a lack of resources, or another colleague's bad attitude, or the company's errant new vision. People under a microscope become very adept at shifting focus to something else.

It requires skill to stay on the subject at hand during important conversations. If you've been in a meeting facilitated by an outside resource, you've probably seen a "parking lot" flip chart. Facilitators use these to skillfully acknowledge and record off-topic issues brought into a conversation while not interrupting the main discussion. Leaders must learn this same skill when having uncomfortable conversations about decisions. Though the other party might bring up important issues to discuss, they can only be addressed after the subject at hand is handled.

It can sound like, "I agree that is another important topic and we need to discuss it, but right now we need to focus on this." Or "Can I write that down so I don't forget to come back to it. I hear how important it is to you but I don't want to get distracted from the importance of this topic right now."

Exercise: Bringing It Together

As you've likely noticed, the four skills work in tandem. Within a conversation, you will employ listening, finding a shared goal, checking your assumptions and bringing it back to the subject at hand.

If you find these skills challenging, try one of the following two exercises:

1. If you are a problem solver who makes a lot of statements, in your next discussion try just asking questions. Not the "Here's what I think you should do" kind of questions like "Have you considered X, Y, and Z?" This is not a question, it's an opinion with a question mark. Tap into your curiosity and Level 2 listening. Practicing this skill in isolation will enable you to be a better influencer.

2. If you are already adept at listening, and struggle with sharing your opinion, practice speaking. Rather than asking another question, make statements. "It sounds like…" or, "I think we should…" Exercise stating your opinion, even if it's premature and not fully formed yet. If it makes you more comfortable, you can add "I'm still assessing, but I believe we should…"

How to Use these Skills to Get Buy-In Early

Having difficult conversations about adherence to a decision is one thing. Getting others on board before a decision is final is quite another. The same tools of shared goals, listening, checking assumptions, and bringing it back to the subject at hand apply to influencing others.

Getting input from key stakeholders long before a decision is made will improve your chances of getting their buy-in. Consider the skills in this way:

- Shared goals: Ask questions to understand what is important to them about this decision. What do they have at stake? What would a win look like for them? Identifying this in your information-gathering stage enables you to do two things. First, you can use it to influence the decision you make and, second, you can use it to discuss shared goals down the road when you need to get them on board with a decision that doesn't look exactly like they had imagined.

- Check your assumptions: When you run through this exercise, you can see what assumptions you hold about the people you need to influence and what assumptions they may hold about you or the context around the decision to be made. By checking these, you will change how you discuss the topic with them, be more successful at finding shared goals and improve your ability to listen to what they are really saying.

- Listening: This skill will serve you well twice: when you are first meeting with people before the decision is made, and when you are sharing the results of the decision. First, employ curiosity when you meet during the information-seeking phase. Make the conversation about them and focus your questions to deepen their thinking, not your understanding of details. Second, when you report on the outcome, leverage listening to understand their concerns and rebuttals. People who feel heard are more likely to reach across the aisle.

- Bringing it back to the subject at hand: As you listen to others' perspectives, especially if you are newly practicing Level 2 listening, it can be easy to let the person talk on and on with little input from you. As an active listener, it is appropriate to table certain topics and redirect the speaker. Simply say, "Forgive my interruption. I'm interested in what you're saying now, but I don't want to lose sight of what you were talking about a minute ago. That seemed really important. Can we go back to that before we go on?" By helping the speaker focus, you will demonstrate both your interest in their opinion and the attention with which you are listening.

These skills will enable you to be a more empathetic partner, in tune with others' interests and able to frame decisions in a way that connects to their expectations. Once you know you're ready to enter the conversation openly, and with the end in mind, it's time to tackle how to manage yourself in the conversation. We'll explore this in the next chapter.

CHAPTER 4

Manage your Brain's Defensive Reactions

Nobody wants to follow someone combative and defensive. Chances are, you've encountered a leader who interprets every question as a challenge and overreacts to small infractions. Likewise, no one wants to get behind the person who's so busy protecting their own agenda that they can't listen to what others have to offer. When it comes to decision making, a defensive stance can stand between you and the supporters who will bring your idea to fruition. To regulate the defensive response, you must first understand what triggers you into it.

Playing Dead in Plain Sight

I was just a few weeks shy of my 21st birthday when I traveled to the Dominican Republic with 29 other college students to begin our three-month semester abroad. It was the late '90s and my feminism was budding. We'd been told that American girls had a reputation as over-sexed partiers (thanks, *MTV Spring Break*) and I wanted to combat that stereotype.

My Spanish was pretty miserable. I'd studied the language for about four years between high school and college and, contrary to what is common, I could speak better than I could understand. Maybe it was an overarching feeling of overwhelm or the speed and unfamiliar accent, but I could not process what they were saying.

My host mom picked me up and it was awkward. She was nice. She'd had lots of students before me. But she didn't make me feel at ease. She had an errand to run on our way to the house. We had to stop by a radio station so she could be interviewed about her dance studio. It might take a while, so I should come in and not wait in the car.

I didn't realize what a big deal this all was until much later. We were whisked into a crowded room. The walls were lined with people, so my host mom and I squished in. In the center were two men sitting at a long table with two large microphones that hung from the ceiling and seemed to take up half the room. We waited. There was talking and laughter and I couldn't understand any of it. When they pulled my host mom in, she was interviewed in rapid-fire Spanish. Suddenly all eyes fell on me. I was pushed toward the mic. My host mom was shaking her head, saying something about how I don't speak Spanish.

My heart rate skyrocketed and the speed of language zooming around me was only a buzz. I knew nothing of what was happening. I picked up the word *"beso."* Kiss. Oh no, they were asking me how many people I've kissed. This was my worst nightmare. I felt I had a responsibility at this moment to single-handedly rewrite the script MTV had imprinted around the world. What's a believable but conservative number? Two? Yes, two it was. *"Dos,"* I squeaked into the microphone. Then the words came faster with more fury—some in Spanish, some in English. I couldn't understand any of it. I kept repeating, *"Si, dos, dos."* Yes, two, two. Laughter erupted. They were not asking me how many people I'd kissed. They were asking me what was the longest I'd ever kissed someone. My doe-eyed *"dos"* was the answer to everything. Two what? Two minutes? *Si, dos.* Two hours? *Si, dos.* Two days? *Si, dos.* Later, when the reality was conveyed to me, I was mortified. Of course, this was not a simple local radio show. This was a show syndicated across all of Latin America. This was the Latin American equivalent of the Howard Stern show. And I had just dropped another quarter in the piggy bank of dumb American girl.

What happened at that moment? Why could I suddenly not even speak English? Why is my heart rate rising even as I type out this story some 20-odd years later? Because there is a subconscious part of my brain screaming, "Not safe! Not safe!" At that moment, I froze. In response to the threat, I did not become aggressive (fight), or run out of the room (flight); I simply played dead (froze).

The Amygdala Hijack

What was happening to me can be described as the "amygdala hijack," a phrase coined by psychologist Daniel Goleman, in his book *Emotional Intelligence*[8], to describe an immediate, overwhelming and instinctive emotional response to threat. In the medial temporal lobe of the brain resides a set of neurons called the amygdala. Part of the limbic system which is responsible for emotions, instinct, and memory, the amygdala is responsible for our fight/flight/freeze reactions. It controls our instinctual defensive responses and it's been critical to our survival since our earliest evolutionary days. It is why people automatically duck when they hear loud noises; it is why parents jump in front of cars to save their children; and it is why I couldn't understand even my own language in that horrible radio story.

The amygdala evolved for our survival. It kicks in before we are conscious of it, but it doesn't work alone. Lower down in our brain sits the brain stem, the most primitive part of our brain. It is constantly, subconsciously, scanning our environment for threats so it can tell the amygdala when to fire off warning signals. Unfortunately, the two together are not very good at distinguishing a physical, life-threatening danger from an emotional one, and therefore the amygdala releases the same fear triggers whether we see a bear or a colleague we don't trust. When activated, our blood rushes to our limbs to enable fighting or fleeing. With our energy surging to our limbs, our prefrontal cortex, where our logic and reasoning happens, becomes underutilized. It's as if we're suddenly dumb and unable to think.

If you've ever found yourself in an emotional argument that you can't quite pull yourself away from, your amygdala has likely triggered a fear response to a threat. Consider the performance review common in most organizations. After months, sometimes even a year, of work, the employee and manager sit down to discuss the employee's performance. The employee's amygdala is triggered before the conversation even begins. It's no wonder that managers and employees alike dread this annual ritual.

When you are nervous, does your heart rate soar? Do your hands get clammy or your mouth dry? Perhaps you sweat or catch yourself holding your breath? These are all physical signs that your amygdala has kicked into a defensive mode.

Like me in the broadcast booth, when the amygdala kicks in, logical thinking is stifled. Reacting to the stimulus in front of us, our ability to make decisions is weakened.

Emotional Stress Makes Us Illogical

When you are under emotional stress, the hardworking brain functions—those responsible for more in-depth problem solving—shut down, and your irrational, let's-figure-out-the-easiest-way-forward function takes over. This function is a notoriously bad decision maker. According to Nobel laureate Daniel Kahneman, who refers to this as "fast thinking" in his book *Thinking Fast and Slow*[9], this function is responsible for our biases and many of the pitfalls commonly cited in books about good decision making. Fast thinking encourages:

- Recency bias: The bias toward information that feels familiar. Even if we know it is untrue, if we hear it repeated, we begin to believe it.

- Anchoring: Considering value for something unknown before estimating the quantity. For example, if asked if there were more than 200 life rafts on the Titanic you will give an answer "anchored" to the number 200. It will differ from your answer to the question, "How many life rafts were on the Titanic?"

- Priming: Recent context "primes" you to think of something associated. If you've seen pictures of food, you will read SO_P as soup, rather than soap.

What this tells us is that we are far less logical than we assume. Emotions can drive our decision making, either through unconscious bias, or through fear-based reactions. If you've ever felt your chest tighten when trying to decide between two good alternatives, you've experienced the amygdala's influence on decision making.

The good news is that there is a way to shrink the amygdala and its impact on your decision making.

Go to Your Happy Place—No, Seriously

Before joining corporate America and becoming a coach and consultant, I served as the program director for a nonprofit retreat center. I created and ran programs that drew a national audience and ran a capital campaign for new program buildings. I was in my late 20s and wrestling with whether or not this was the career I wanted to build. I'd also spent the decade figuring out how to run budgets and manage people. Though wildly helpful in building my cross-functional thinking qualities, my liberal arts English degree had given me no direct skills in finance or management. I knew I wanted to go to graduate school, but I was unsure where, when, or how. Looking back, it feels like an easy decision but, in that moment, it was tormenting me. I was regularly in a heightened emotional state, unsure of how to make the decision, wracked with guilt at the thought of leaving programming that I had created, yet drawn toward a new chapter.

Luckily, I worked among beautiful trails and hills and woods. I took to foot and hiked toward a clearing overlooking the Laurel Highlands in Western Pennsylvania.

Nature has always given me perspective. Whether back-packing, or simply sitting by a lake, I always feel put in my place in nature. The entire ecosystem hangs in balance. Each organism plays its role and the system responds in kind. The oak produces acorns, which the squirrel then gathers and buries and forgets about, which grow into new trees. Not much thinking required there. Sitting by old limestone boulders, I'm reminded that they are ancient and that I am a blip in the Earth's history. It gives me perspective. It doesn't always answer my question, but it always calms my nerves.

Vaishali Mamgain, an economics professor at the University of Southern Maine and Executive Director of the Bertha Crosley Ball Center for Compassion, has researched the neuroscience behind mindfulness and compassion. Her research revealed a simple meditation that can pull you out of an amygdala hijack in mere minutes. By simply imagining yourself in a familiar natural space, you can reduce the amygdala's foothold. It's become a cultural cliché, but going to your happy place can really work.

Fascinatingly, research has shown that meditation can shrink the amygdala, in turn reducing the amount of time it spends triggering our fear responses. As reported in Scientific American[10], MRI scans conducted before and after participation in an eight-month meditation program showed a physical decrease in the size of participants' amygdala. When the amygdala gets smaller, the prefrontal cortex thickens, and the connectivity between the amygdala and the primitive parts of the brain weakens. This means that, even when the primitive brain sends a warning signal of potential threat, the amygdala is slower to fire off defensive reactions.

Repeated use of meditation, and mind-settling tools like the ones I share below, are like exercise for your logical brain. As you teach your brain to react less to emotional threats, the amygdala shrinks in size and loses its influence on you. By learning to settle the mind, we improve our ability to make decisions from a rational and logical place.

Protective reactions impact your decision making in two ways:

1. They shut down your logical brain, and cause emotion-based fear, which has been shown to reduce effective decision making.

2. They prevent you from influencing others by creating communication barriers.

Simply put, until you learn to manage the natural defensive reactions that we all experience, your success is in jeopardy.

Exercises to Shrink Your Amygdala

Meditation can take many forms, from silent, clear-your-mind transcendental meditation, to walking a path in a meditative state. Once reserved as a spiritual practice, meditation has become commonplace in organizations, as leaders discover the impact a calm mind has on employee productivity. Leaders can now readily find apps, books, and classes to deepen their understanding of, and ability to practice, meditation. The following exercises will help you dip your toe in meditation. To shrink your amygdala, you will need to find the right meditation style for you and practice with regularity.

Exercise One: Imagine a Natural Setting

Sit comfortably in your chair, both feet firmly on the floor, your back supported by your chair. Close your eyes and breathe in and out three times. Feel the breath move into your limbs, then focus on the exhale. The inhale to exhale length should be a one-to-three ratio.

Imagine a beautiful place in nature that feels like home to you. It should be familiar. Someplace you have spent time, that feels comfortable. It does not need to be a wild place, just a natural one. Imagine yourself there. See the sky and the vegetation. Feel the air on your skin. Smell the familiar scents. Hear the surrounding sounds. If your mind wanders, notice the thoughts without judging yourself and come back to the image of your natural place. Spend 90 seconds in this visualization.

After the exercise, notice how your body feels. Have you relaxed? What impact did it have on your mind or the "ticker tape" of thoughts? Were you able to maintain focus or did your mind wander? Intruding thoughts are common, especially when meditation is new. Repeat this exercise as often as you like. Try increasing the time to three minutes, then five.

Exercise Two: Exercise with Intention

If you are someone who struggles with focus while being still, exercising with intention can be a useful tool. Whether going outside for a walk or run, or heading to the gym, choose a workout that is strenuous and that will require you to focus on your physical work, not something that you can do absentmindedly while getting lost in thoughts. Walking is okay, but choose a fast pace to keep your mind focused.

Before your workout, set an intention or question. You may choose to write it down. Keep it simple. A few examples of intentions and questions are: I'm going to be present and not worry about what I don't know. What is my indecision really about? I'm going to challenge myself to go harder without judging my current state. How am I really feeling about this decision?

After your workout, set a timer for five to ten minutes and answer the question, or reflect on the intention.

Exercise Three: Connecting with Your Five Senses

When you notice that you feel anxious or distracted, this exercise is a quick and simple way to refocus your attention. It only takes about 30 seconds. You simply work your way through your five senses, stopping to notice each thing before moving to the next.

1. Five things you see: Notice each one briefly, before moving to the next. Look for unusual things that you might not always pay attention to.

2. Four things you feel: This could be the clothes touching your skin, your feet in your shoes, or your legs against the chair.

3. Three things you hear: In a quiet setting, you may need to pay attention to the white noise that you often ignore.

4. Two things you smell: Breathe deeply to find them. Breathe in with intention.

5. One thing you taste: You can swallow or take a drink of a beverage near you.

How do You Know You're in a Defensive State?

Most often, we move through life unaware of our current emotional state until it reaches an elevated level like anger, frustration, or elation. But, at any given time, we are somewhere on an emotional scale. As adults, many of us spend a good bit of time in a calm and focused state. Some of us have a higher threshold for input, and might function at a higher energy level than others. No matter our preferred state, we all have a "normal" that we generally calibrate to. When we significantly deviate from that normal, we're very aware of it. It is the smaller deviations that we are often unaware of, and that lead to the bigger deviations.

I'm sure you've woken up on the wrong side of the bed. You might be aware that you're more agitated than usual but, often, you wouldn't even name it until someone else lets you know that you're operating with a short fuse. If we're emotionally attuned, we can check in and recognize it. If not, we might snap at the person calling our attention to it, and then go about our day, functioning at a different energy level than is our normal.

When this happens, our interactions with others change. My friend tells a great story about a leader whose administrative assistant created a system for letting others know whether or not the boss was in an approachable mood. A green folder on the corner of the desk meant to go on in; a red folder meant to proceed with caution. Chances are, this leader was unaware of how much impact his emotional state was having on business. His team was choosing to delay business decisions based on the boss's emotions.

Like a poker player who unconsciously gives indicators about the cards he's holding, we all have emotional "tells" that can clue us in to our emotional state. To identify yours, recall a story that you associate with negative emotion. For me, the story of the Dominican Republic at the beginning of this chapter is a great example. Pick a story where there's some element of embarrassment—either now or when the event occurred. Tell the story in your head, or aloud. As you recount the story, pay attention to what is physically happening in your body. Some common physical sensations are shallow breathing, sweaty palms, red or hot neck or cheeks, twisting gut and a sweaty forehead. What you are feeling right now are the physical tells that you are in a deviated emotional state.

You can teach yourself to notice these "tells" before you've even logically register that something is off. If someone suggests you're grumpy, you can probably locate a sensation of agitation somewhere in your body. Rather than snapping back, consider that it might be true, recognize the physical sensation and recalibrate. Sometimes, simply pausing to consider whether or not you are agitated can bring you back into your thinking brain.

A Note on Intuition

It seems that I'm suggesting that the only good decision making is rational and researched, and that our intuitive natures are irrational and faulty. Yes and no. Because we've been taught to be rational and logical, we learn to discount anything that we can't think our way into. It's worth exploring this a little further, armed with knowledge about our defensive reactions.

We often experience gut feelings as fear. (And, in fact, research now shows that the primitive brain stem is connected to the gut[11]. The gut and the primitive brain work together to detect threat.) Many gut reactions are fear-based and prevent us from acting. This doesn't mean that a gut sense is inherently bad. You might get a gut sense not to do something that is worth heeding. It is, however, critical to understand that gut senses come from a place of caution. Knowing this enables you to assess if the fear is warranted.

Different from the gut response, some thoughts come like bursts of lightning and feel inspired. Because we often feel this physically, in our heart-centers, I call this "heart sense." It is connected to our values, dreams and creativity. This is our intuition working in flow.

When intuition hits, we often approach it with caution because we've been taught that the only good thought is one we've searched for, never one that's found us. However, some of the world's best thinkers, entrepreneurs, and business leaders rely on intuition. Bill Gates, Steve Jobs, Oprah Winfrey, Albert Einstein, and countless others all credit intuition as critical to their success.

Intuition is a skill to be developed with the sister-skill of discernment. You might get an intuitive idea that is not currently feasible, and therefore not the right decision.

Consider a manager who has a sudden thought that he should restructure his team. If the new system would improve employees' experience or productivity (building on something good to make it better), it might be an intuitive interruption and worth considering. It might also be the case that a restructure would inflict emotional turmoil on the team, which would slow down progress on a critical project.

How, then, to determine if the intuition is helpful? Notice where you feel the intuitive response. Is it in your gut and cautionary? Or is it in your heart and visionary? If it is a gut sense, what is the concern? If it is a heart sense, what would it take to follow it? What is your emotional state? Are you in a state of worry? Are you calm and rested?

Your curiosity (using the listening skills from the previous chapter) will also benefit you here. Fear is a trickster and will try to show up as intuition to direct you away from something that requires great courage. Knowing that about fear is important. So is learning to sort out the competing voices we all have in our heads. More on that in Chapter Six.

Before we can get to the real power of intuition, we need to explore the barriers standing between you and excellent decision making.

PART 2

REMOVING THE OBSTACLES TO DECISION MAKING

CHAPTER 5

Reinvent Your Role and Expectations

The Perils of Overperforming

I was working with a risk management team in a financial institution several years ago. The group was made up of auditors and leaders directly involved in the day-to-day decision making within the business. As you can imagine, business leaders don't like being told by auditors that they are doing something risky. Business leaders wanted to be counseled on their risk profile, not stripped of all risk. The audit professionals prided themselves on their independence and reputation with the regulators. This created a bit of an impasse.

In my decade-long experience with financial institutions, I've learned that there is one commonality universal in the financial industry: high achievers. These folks want to get straight As. When I taught Gallup's StrengthsFinder in this industry, "achiever" was such a frequent "Top 5" strength that it became a joke. If it didn't show up in your "Top 5", you might not last long!

The aha moment in the room happened when the auditors collectively realized they were trying to be exemplar students for the regulator, at the expense of the actual risk interests of the bank. This was not a call to abandon risk protocols, but rather to collectively agree that an A- was a good grade, and that striving for an A+ was too costly. If they worked together for an A-, the business would be more likely to bring forward concerns, and the auditors would be more likely to look for solutions.

Often, high achievers fall into this A+ trap. We strive to be the best, and assume that is what everyone is expecting of us when, in fact, it's a standard that exhausts, overwhelms, and burns us out. Every time I see a client step into a new role with elevated leadership requirements, they wrestle with accepting the mantra of "good enough" instead of "perfect."

Perfect Is the Enemy of Good

Voltaire said, "The perfect is the enemy of the good," and this concept has been used by philosophers throughout history. It means that striving for perfection can prevent you from achieving anything at all, as seen in the previous example. In every aspect of our lives this dysfunction shows up as we assume several roles (parent, executive, teacher, engineer, creative, etcetera) and set high standards for performing each one. It influences how we make decisions because we search for the perfect solution, or future course of action. This desire for excellence sets you up for a high-pressure life. You've heard the pressure cooker metaphor before: if the container isn't safe, it's deadly. The contents can only survive under intense pressure for so long without exploding. Eventually, you need a release valve.

When you are in the pressure cooker of trying to be perfect (or even good!) at everything, you will not make good decisions. Multiple stressors impact our mood. It is quite difficult to feel the pressure and remain in a calm and positive mood. In their 2003 article, in *Psychological Science*[12], a group of German scientists reported the effect that mood has on intuitive responses. In their study, they discovered that when we are in a foul mood, our intuitive senses are no better than random answers. When in a good mood, however, our intuitive responses are far better than a random selection. When we are in a pleasant mood, we have better cognitive ease. Not only does the pressure cooker not feel good, it is stressing out your brain and impeding your decision-making abilities.

Have a go at the following exercise to explore whether you are suffering from your own unreachable standards, and how this affects your decision making. Get out a pen and paper and spend a few minutes thinking about your answers to each question.

1. What does being in charge mean to you?

2. What does being right mean?

3. How do you know you're right?

4. What roles in your life (work and beyond) require you to be in charge?

5. What roles in your life require you to make decisions?

6. On a one-to-ten scale, how important is it that your decisions are good in each of those roles?

If you have anything above a six in three or more roles, you are living in a pressure cooker and it is impeding your decision making. The rest of this chapter is about how to find your release valve.

Naming and Claiming Your Roles

We all have roles in many places in our lives: parent, executive, coach, creative, artist, engineer. These roles influence the decision-making pressure we are under.

Take a moment to identify your roles. They might look like this:

- Father
- Executive
- Business leader
- Soccer coach
- Husband

- Engineer
- Provider
- Rock

Perhaps, as the exercise went on, and your list lengthened, the roles shifted a bit. As you can see in my example list, there are roles that everyone can see, and then there are roles that we internalize. Because you are a father or husband, you might feel the expectations to be a provider or rock. Here's where the desire for the A+ grade starts to weigh us down. We assume that others' expectations of us are to be perfect in each of those roles. I'm here to tell you that that is impossible. You cannot be perfect at each of those things. Those who appear to be perfect are in the pressure cooker, with the power cranked up, scorching everything inside. So, what are you to do when everyone with a stake in each of those areas *does* expect pretty high performance? That's where your ability to choose comes in to play.

Some of our roles come, often unintentionally, due to our gender and status. And most of these roles come with our and others' expectations or "baggage." Some baggage is beautiful and designer and newly picked out—that's great. Some baggage is worn and tired and tethered to our ankles, just following us around and slowing us down. Sorting out which variety of baggage you have is critical to decision making. You are most likely unaware of it and it is impacting how you make decisions (check back in on Chapter Four for more on the neuroscience here.) Look at your role list. Have you included any assigned to you based on gender or status? If not, add those in.

Now that you have a healthy list of roles, it's time to list all the expectations under those roles. For each role, write down expectations you have for yourself, or that others have of you. For example:

- Father: present, calm, disciplinarian, play, available.
- Executive: bold, confident, funny, smart, right, intuitive, decisive.
- Business leader: compassionate, hard, tough talking, inventive, visionary, leader.
- Soccer coach: fun, knowledgeable, available, in charge, planner, cruise ship director, cat herder, patient.
- Husband: present, listener, provider, unemotional, problem solver, fixer, handyman.
- Engineer: logical, analytical, thorough, smart, careful.
- Provider: earner, advancing, stable, planning, managing, accountant, omniscient.
- Rock: stoic, unmoving, unemotional, even-keel.

You'll notice some stereotypes in my examples. The words may not hold for you. They may not be expectations you have of that role, but they may relate to others' expectations of you. Stereotypes mean that people in society carry some expectations of you based on that role, as outdated as they may be. If you are a husband, some people believe that you should be stoic and provide. If you are a mother, some people believe that you should manage the household's calendar and bear the mental load of running a family. Even my clients who very intentionally choose not to take on those expectations in their roles, find that they are still aware of those stereotypes, and they sometimes work against them in the background. I encourage you to examine both the stereotypes you buy into and those you reject.

When you've created your list, look it over. If you are like every single one of my clients, it will be easy to see why you might feel overwhelmed and ready to embrace the midlife crisis. My high-achieving clients hold a lot of high expectations for themselves. They take on a lot of high expectations from others. Some of these are true and nonnegotiable, but fewer than you might think.

Redefining Your Roles

When we assume a role and its expectations, sometimes we are taking on beliefs and perspectives that have been passed down. You might have learned from your parents what it means to be a mother or father, a husband or wife, an executive. You saw it in your earliest years and you learned to imitate it. You did this naturally, unconsciously. It was good for you at that time.

When you look at your list, which expectations are you tired of? Which feel unfair? Which cause some agitation when you read them? Circle them. Believe it or not, you have a choice in this matter. You can decide you no longer want to be the omniscient provider. Maybe you're okay with being the earner, but trying to be all-knowing is unrealistic and unhelpful. If it feels like a weight on your shoulders, I promise you that it is impacting your ability to make good decisions. You can continue to tough it out and slog through, or you can renegotiate these expectations—some of which might be your own—and decide to live only with roles and expectations that you willingly accept.

Examining our roles and expectations, and being willing to have potentially uncomfortable conversations to renegotiate them, is critical. It is not a nice-to-have; it is a need-to-have. You will not improve your decision making if the pressure has been on high for too long. You will function at a lower mental level, suffering from both decision fatigue and lower executive function. Simple decisions will feel confusing. To make authentic decisions, you will need to engage in redefining your roles.

A Story of Mismatched Expectations

A friend of mine, who is now a successful consultant and coach, was once an academic promoted to dean of a department. He's whip-smart, a quick study, and dedicated to excellence, making him a great selection to lead, except he'd never led a group of people before.

Among many of the assumptions new leaders make, one of the biggest has to do with decision making. Leaders receive requests for help, and for decisions, in astonishing numbers. New leaders believe that everything that comes their way is theirs to solve. After all, most leaders were put in place because they were excellent problem solvers, so the expectations of them in their new role, they assume, must be the same.

For my friend, this meant making every decision that came across his desk with speed and certainty. He kept a log of the decisions in queue, and his goal was to keep the queue in check. The quicker he decided, the more manageable the backlog became, he reasoned. It was a logical process but, being new in his role, he did not yet know the impact his decisions would have on others. He saw his decisions in isolation, not as part of a system with broader effects.

It didn't take long to realize the results of unilateral decision making. He found himself backtracking when his staff informed him of the downstream effect his decisions created. Rather than being seen as a decisive and thorough decision maker, he became someone who had to reverse his hasty decisions.

He initially took on all of the responsibility, shared none of the load, and asked for no counsel, believing that asking for help would make him appear weak. He believed that doing it himself was the expectation of the role. Luckily for him, he has strong emotional intelligence and quickly realized he needed to change. He revised his assumptions about the role and even changed the role itself—he was not decider-in-chief, he was collaborator-in-chief. He was responsible for making sure a good decision was made, but not responsible for making it independently.

Exercise: Get Out of Your Head

If this role work feels uncomfortable, difficult, or you find yourself relying too much on analytical thinking, and not enough on your intuitive thinking, this exercise can help you access your right brain and encourage creative thinking.

Grab a pen and several sheets of paper or a journal:

1. Write a simple question about your role, or the unnamed expectations, such as, "What role am I overfunctioning in?" Then ignore the question for the next part of the exercise.

2. Walk around, preferably outside, until you find a plant that draws your eye. If you are inside, look for a house plant. Whether in or out, find something living that your eye is drawn to. Set a timer for ten minutes and sketch this plant—maybe part of it, maybe all of it. Take your time. It does not matter how good your sketch is,

but take the full ten minutes and pay attention to details that you notice.

3. When the timer rings, set another timer for ten minutes and journal an answer to your question. Keep writing for the full ten minutes. If you run out of ideas, simply write, "I don't know what to say," and write about that for a while.

Once you've assessed your assumed roles, and renegotiated (sometimes with yourself) what you do and don't want, you'll be ready to tackle the mental tickertape of conflicting ideas running through your head. In the next chapter, we'll explore strategies to deal with the "back-and-forth" of decision making.

CHAPTER 6

Stop the Back-and-Forth

No Decision is Right or Wrong

I had to hire a graphic designer for a significant project I was working on. It was a project I had invested a substantial amount of money into and needed to give it every shot at winning, including a killer look that made it stand out. I put together my brief, asked friends and colleagues for referrals, and searched online for high-quality designers who could think strategically with me, not get lost in their love of white space. I needed form and function.

I had a great list of designers to interview. I pored over their portfolios, scrutinized how they presented themselves, tested them to see who both understood my vision and challenged me to think bigger. After narrowing it down to three, I got consumed by other urgent business matters like ordering new business cards. Suddenly I felt busier than I'd felt in a while. I was just too busy each day to make the decision on who to hire.

I'm a decision-making coach and it took me several days to recognize what I was doing. If you recognize this game, know you're in good company! I was no busier than I'd been the previous week. I was inventing busyness to put off making a decision I wasn't sure how to make. I had three great designers to choose from. While I could envision different outcomes from each of them, no single path would steer me in a direction I couldn't recover from. I really couldn't make a bad choice, just a different choice.

When faced with several good options, it would seem that making a decision should come easily, but in fact it is the opposite. Even when there are few relatively "bad" choices, we still revert to our inner analyzer and high achiever, convinced we are capable of finding the singular best answer among similar choices. We go over all the data multiple times, weighing options and possible outcomes. When we eventually make a choice, convinced we've been logical and thorough, others criticize the length of time it took us to reach our conclusion.

Coach training challenged my right/wrong, find-the-best-answer brain. I remember sitting in a circle with all the other coaches in training. We were asked to apply a lens that assumed everything spoken, as either client or coach during the workshop, was right. "Does that mean everything gets to be right, no matter how ridiculous?" I thought to myself. I imagined Oprah here handing out "You're right!" cards—"And you get to be right! And you get to be right!" It's a bizarre notion, isn't it? That any choice could be right? We are trained to believe that there is a critical path. Shifting to see any choice as right seems nonsensical.

Yet, if you remove right/wrong thinking, you can see that any choice can be defended and every choice will have a consequence. Some of those consequences will be favorable, and some unfavorable. Just like in my story about auditors in Chapter Five, we cannot eliminate the risk that a decision will have unintended consequences. Most high-achieving decision makers work hard to analyze and eliminate as much risk as possible, but risk is not necessarily predictable. When we take care to analyze all of our options, it is because we are looking for the good and right. The problem is not that we don't want to make a decision (most of the time), it's that we assume (here we are, back to assuming expectations and roles) that our job is to weigh everything precisely and choose the option that is as close to risk-free as possible. Not only is this impossible, it's not even logical. We hold these choices against each other as though it is gospel truth that there is only one good choice. In actuality, no decision is purely right or wrong, good or bad. We must understand the causality between choice and outcome, and recognize our own expectation of what is "right" in order to make authentic decisions.

Overanalyzing our options like this can lead to back-and-forth decision making. We can get in trouble with two different types of back-and-forth obstacles to flow: being caught in a pendulum swing where we make one decision and then renege on it and make the opposite decision, or wavering back and forth, unable to land on the best choice.

Obstacle One: The Pendulum Swing

I once worked with a clinical care center. As is common in health-related businesses, this organization had a clear divide between the clinical staff—those who saw and treated patients directly - and the administrative staff, who managed records and paid attention to the behind-the-scenes systems. "We must adhere to policies and procedures at all costs," said the administrators. "But it is getting in the way of the patient experience," said the clinicians. If you've been to a doctor's office lately, you've probably experienced this tension. It is common for a nurse or doctor to face a computer screen while asking personal questions, perhaps about a serious health concern. It solves record management, but it is a horrible patient experience. You've also likely heard of HIPAA violations, where a provider is so connected to patient experience that they don't properly store records and information gets shared inappropriately. In the argument between patient or record primacy, neither side is purely right, and neither side is purely wrong.

Management struggled with this ongoing tension. When they took the side of the administration, and clamped down on efficient record keeping and use of internal systems, there was a noticeable increase in patient complaints, and the clinical team started to get overwhelmed and take more time off. Reacting to this, management then swung the pendulum in the other direction, but this created chaos for the administrative department.

Though we see these entities laid out as opposites, the administrative and clinical sides of the house are interdependent. You cannot prioritize one at the expense of another without getting caught in an ongoing pendulum swing. Barry Johnson has developed an entire process for what he labels "polarity management." "Polarities to manage are sets of opposites that can't function well independently," he explains. "Because the two sides of a polarity are interdependent, you cannot choose one as a 'solution' and neglect the other.[13]" To hold both as right, and both as wrong, we need to see them from a high enough perspective to understand their interdependence.

Consider the clinic's clinical/administrative polarity. There are upsides and downsides to both poles.

The upside of a clinical focus includes a focus on the patient, listening, caring relationships, referrals, and better diagnoses. But there is also a downside to "solving" the problem with a clinical focus: poor patient data management, HIPAA violations, disorganized records leading to poor follow-up care, and sparse documentation that can hide unethical behaviors.

Of course, the same is true of the administrative "solution." The upside includes careful recordkeeping, policies protecting both patients and institutional reputation, securing patients' trust that their privacy is protected, accurate and timely billing and follow-up, and care continuity between specialties. But the downsides include burdensome procedures that impede doctor/patient connection, inflexible hierarchy, red tape that slows down care, impersonal service, and overworked clinicians.

Both upsides are necessary for a high-functioning department. Though each side holds competing priorities, they must be managed together to experience the upsides of both, and limit the downsides of both.

I've seen pendulum swings in countless organizations. From centralized to decentralized, hierarchical to matrixed, collaborative to autonomous. Each of these is an example of an interdependent polarity. When you choose one over the other, you temporarily get the upside, but quickly also experience the downside. This causes people to desire the other pole and swing the pendulum back, only to find themselves back in another downside. There is a third option that avoids choosing one pole and then vacillating back-and-forth at a later date. The option is to find a solution that satisfies both sides of the argument, blending their priorities and discouraging a pendulum swing.

Leaders must become wary of decisions posed as opposites and test whether or not the two choices are interdependent. Focusing on either customer engagement or sales is a polarity to manage because they are interdependent. If asked to choose between polarities, you need to ask more questions and explore the upsides and downsides of both to help others see the risk of a pendulum swing.

Obstacle Two: Competing Inner Voices

When talking about decisions, I regularly hear clients say, "Well, part of me thinks this, but part of me thinks that." This is normal! To explore options from a broad perspective, we need to understand the parts at play within our thinking. These are our competing "inner voices."

The easiest way to understand this is to begin with everyone's favorite guy to hate: the inner critic. If you have not encountered your inner critic, you might be a psychopath and you are reading the wrong book. Psychopaths have no remorse or moral compass and the inner critic feeds on both of those things. The inner critic is that little (or not so little) voice that causes you to doubt yourself. In the land of decision making, it says things like, "This is a terrible decision. What are you thinking? Who do you think you are to make a decision this big? You haven't analyzed this enough. You need more research. You are in no way prepared for this. Even if you make this choice, you can't pull this off. You'll never sell this idea." You get the picture. The inner critic is alive and well in most of us.

In my early years as a coach, I learned to call this the voice of the saboteur, and to help clients dismiss it. After working with clients with some pretty pesky and adept saboteurs, I've developed a new relationship with this prevalent voice. I've since learned that this new strategy is backed up by the research of Richard Schwartz and Internal Family Systems (IFS) therapy[14]. According to Schwartz, in his book *Introduction to the Internal Family Systems Model*, when we say, "Part of me thinks this, but part of me thinks that," we are recognizing the rival arguments that we play out in our heads regularly.

I like to think of these as the competing voices in our head and, rest assured, this does not make you schizophrenic; it makes you human. The angel and devil on the shoulder are one of the oldest tropes in fiction and a great example of two parts of ourselves competing for attention.

Consider my decision over which designer to choose, to see these parts at play, almost like a script in my head. There's a visionary at play who wants to go big, there's a cautious CFO who's concerned with cost, and there's an inner critic who thinks I'm taking too big a risk. The internal dialogue might sound something like this:

Visionary voice: Our future rests on this and we need to go big. This could reach so many people, and it needs to visually reflect our readiness for that.

CFO voice: Perhaps. But it's a big expense and some of these people are a little more affordable because they're just starting out. Let's choose them to hedge our bets.

Visionary voice: Are you kidding? This is too big to chance to some unknown. We don't deserve to win if we aren't willing to play.

Inner critic voice: I don't think this risk is worth taking. We should scrap the project altogether because it will expose us to criticism.

CFO voice: That's a good point. Why don't we wait a few months until we know if the big project closes so we can pad our cash flow first.

As funny as it seems to lay this out like a script, this is what we do all day with decisions, large and small. We lay out competing arguments and, to find the single best solution, we try to poke holes in the options we're considering. We really shouldn't worry about whether or not others judge us because we are masterful at taking care of that ourselves!

Sometimes the internal back-and-forth gets loud enough that we want to shut them up so we can just make a decision already. If the choice is inconsequential, we'll do some quick analysis and make a decision, feeling good about the thorough diagnostics we applied. But, when we consider a more complex decision with more serious consequences, the voices have much more to say and they don't go away as easily.

In my work with clients who are wrestling with competing decisions, rather than tuning out the voices, we engage with them to understand what each is representing. By getting these voices out of the ticker tape in our heads, we can better understand what is at stake in each choice, and decide from a place of integrity and confidence.

To explore what this looks like in practice and its impact on decision making, let's take the inner critic voice.

Imagine that your critic is a character and it has opinions and desires. It wants to be heard. The higher the stakes, the louder and more argumentative it gets. If we hide it in the corner, it shouts. It might disguise itself as something else to get our attention. It's an adept character. You probably have some disdain for it.

Now imagine yourself, not as the person who is the victim of the inner critic, but as the counselor of the inner critic, who respects it and seeks to understand its perspective, even when disagreeing with it. A counselor might say, "Help me see why this is important to you." The counselor will listen. The counselor might still have some teaching to do and say, "I understand better what your concerns are. Thank you for being honest. Here's how I see it."

These voices are like little seven-year-olds running around in our heads. They have really strong opinions and lack the knowledge we've built over the years. They don't get to call the shots but, when they feel heard and understood by an adult, they are better at accepting a decision that they don't understand.

The key to sorting out our voices is to see them through caring eyes, not the frustrated judgmental eyes that we typically see with. In other words, stop exiling your inner critic and start caring about it, and you will change the power it has over you.

When we shut down our inner voices, they get louder and trickier and try new tactics until they succeed at getting our attention.

In Chapter Three, I shared tools for listening and suggested that people have a deep need to be heard. So it is with your inner voices. They need to know that you are listening. The irony is that they don't always care if you follow their advice, so long as they feel heard. They are almost always a voice of fear about some undesirable outcome. If you can understand what they are worried about, you can help assuage the fear.

When you feel conflicted about decisions, the following exercise is helpful to get clear on what opinions are coming from where.

Exercise: Hold a Board Meeting with Your Inner Voices

Isolate each competing voice that has an opinion about your decision. Give each voice a name. You might have the inner critic, the security guard, the daredevil, and the pragmatist as examples. Sometimes you only need to pay attention to one prominent voice; sometimes you will need to engage several. Go as in-depth as necessary until you feel less pressure mounting.

Once you've identified the members on your team, hold a board meeting.

In this meeting, you are a neutral facilitator talking to a team who each play one of these roles. Hear each of them out. Your task is not to take the advice of every team member, but to hear their side of the story, listen for their concerns and ensure that they feel heard and considered by the end of the meeting.

If you find yourself judging or being irritated by any team member, remember that you are the neutral facilitator and your only task is to listen and understand. You do not need to heed their counsel.

Pulling It Together

Competing options and competing inner voices stand in the way of clear and quick decision making. The skill of managing polarities, when practiced regularly, can become second nature to the decision maker. Interdependent choices become immediately recognizable and can be explored as such. Competing choices in your head can be seen as inner voices with opinions to air. They can be given time to unload and become less burdensome on the decision-making process. Both take time and effort to master, and both are critical to becoming a wise decision maker.

When you're able to manage these competing choices and voices, you're ready to tackle the stories you've been telling yourself about what you are (and are not) capable of. We'll look at strategies to handle this problem in the next chapter.

CHAPTER 7

Get Over the Stories of Past Failure

You Are What You Think

"Sit there and think about what you did," we tell children. We want them to feel the effect of their actions and assume guilt and remorse for the disappointment they've caused. Those are all lessons we must learn as we grow up; our actions have consequences, and we have choices in preventing the unwanted outcome. The problem is that it is also the root of shame. We are all still thinking about what we did days, months and even years later. We take that lesson to "Sit there and think about what you did," and we do it over and over and over, internalizing it as a core part of our very identity.

"I'm not a good communicator," my client Jason told me. He'd been given the feedback enough times that he believed it to be true. When under pressure, he had a tendency to worry about the worst possible outcomes and steel himself against it. This came out as aggressive retorts and defensive repetition of key points he wanted to ensure others understood. Every time he was given feedback on this pattern, he'd resort to the "I'm a bad communicator" line.

Jason had some communication challenges, but his bigger issue was that he'd internalized it as an identity, something fixed and immoveable. As we worked together, I paid special attention to catch him doing something right. When he communicated with nuance, I praised him. When he acknowledged his anxiety rather than lashing out, I helped him see the growth he was demonstrating. Over time, Jason was able to shift his own belief about what he was and was not capable of.

We all fall into the trap of internalizing the feedback or reprimands we get from others. We are also all guilty of giving feedback in a way that causes people to believe *they* are the thing we are criticizing. The way we talk with people reinforces their identity messages. But this chapter isn't about the impact you have on others. This one is all about you and recognizing those stories that you've internalized.

I'm not talking about your guilt for wrongdoing. Your acknowledgment of bad choices or errors is a good thing. What I'm talking about is the internalization of those actions. The shift from "I did a bad thing" to "I am bad." I'm talking about shame.

Shame Is the Decision Maker's Antagonist

Shame cripples our ability to make decisions because it would have us believe that we are no good at them.

I can speak from experience here. I have built a business, teaching corporate leaders, sometimes 20-plus years my senior. I've led Fortune 50 executives through strategy sessions. I've brought grown men to tears, as they unpack the obstacles standing in their way. I have accomplished some pretty remarkable things. Yet the shame that I picked up earlier in my career can still haunt me, and I am constantly listening for its voice so I can help it step out of my way. You'll recognize from the previous chapter that it can show up as your inner critic. Part of the work is treating it as such, not just sending it to the corner to sit there and think about what it did!

After grad school, I jumped from the nonprofit world straight into corporate America. I went from being a big fish in a small pond to a very little fish in a very big pond. I still saw myself as a big fish. Big fish in big ponds are not very kind to little fish with big-fish personalities. Someone once told me that my confidence made people "want to beat it out of me." Ouch.

I could have taken the feedback and learned to work around others. I could have said, "To hell with this place

I'll go somewhere that appreciates my talents." What I did instead was to become the small fish they expected me to be. I shrank. I took the smaller jobs they gave me. I sat in there and thought about what I did. I took on the shame that I couldn't be successful. I became someone who failed.

Lest you think I became meek, know this: as the months dragged on and I tried to fit into their box, I became a pain in the ass to be around. I was miserable and others knew it. People I worked closely with knew it, my boss knew it, my husband knew it, my friends knew it. I was going to get out of there and I had an escape plan. I was going to start my own company and show them all! I was going to kill it!

I had plenty of hustle, but I still had internalized shame. That identity of failing in corporate America, of being someone that people wanted to beat something out of— that wore me like an old pair of jeans. I'd try to sell my coaching and consulting, but I did not show up like someone who could stand in front of a room, even though I had done it with ease plenty of times. Instead, I showed up as someone wearing the shame of being too big. I showed up small and with none of the swagger I once had. I wanted so much to succeed, but I could not succeed because of the shame I wore. The more I failed, the more I took on that identity. The more rejection, the further I retreated to the corner to sit there and think about what I did.

I couldn't make decisions on strategy, marketing or on networking because I didn't believe I was capable of it. I wish I could tell you that I had an aha moment and someone shook me out of it, but that's not how it happened. It took years for me to unlearn.

Here's what shame does to decision making: it triggers the amygdala by making you believe you aren't safe. That fear diverts resources from your thinking, analyzing and processing brain functions. Trying to make decisions from an amygdala hijack like this is almost impossible. And your amygdala will be triggered over and over again, until you deal with the shame. You will not get better at decision making as long as you let shame have a home. You can read all the books, by all the experts, on processes and mental models and they will get you nowhere as long as shame shuts off your ability to process.

Brené Brown is a shame researcher whose books have taught millions of people the courageous power of vulnerability. Here is her shame 101 from *Dare to Lead*[15]:

1. We all have it. Shame is universal and one of the most primitive human emotions that we experience. The only people who don't experience shame are those who lack the capacity for empathy and human connection.

2. We're all afraid to talk about shame. Just the word is uncomfortable.

3. The less we talk about shame, the more control it has over our lives.

We all harbor shame. The process of transforming your shame is some of the most important work you will do. As you learn to let it go, you will find your decision-making flow.

Rewriting the Story

Remember "nothing is good or bad" from Chapter Six? It applies here. Yes, actions can be good or bad from a moral sense, but *you* are neither. And you are both.

When we hear lies in repetition, even when we aren't confident in their validity, we start to believe them to be true.[16] This is why emotional abusers are so adept at gaslighting, verbal shaming and put-downs. As their victims hear the abusive statements repeated, they start to believe them.

If this is true, that we believe things we hear in repetition, then it must be true that we can reverse the beliefs by hearing the opposite in repetition. Some of you will remember the comical "Daily Affirmations with Stuart Smalley", Al Franken's SNL character from the '90s, saying, "I'm good enough, I'm smart enough, and doggone it, people like me!" While I don't expect you to spend time looking in the mirror, giving yourself pep talks, there is something to this technique! Here are the other tropes it goes by:

- "Fake it till you make it"
- "Dress for the job you want"
- "Let people see you doing the job of a level above you"
- "Talk like an expert and people will believe you"

Successful leaders have been doing this for years. Here's the catch: you can't successfully do it outwardly, if you haven't done it inwardly.

Leaders, trying to "fake it till they make it" can come across as fake and untrustworthy if they don't actually believe they can do the job they are hustling for. So, how are we supposed to shake the shame if we can't just shake it off? The only way out is through, my friend. And we're going to do this together.

Exercise: Rewriting the Stories That Stick

Before we can rewrite our stories of shame into stories of learning, we need to examine the lies these stories are telling us. The reason it took me years to recover, is that I thought I could just put on some armor and go out there without staring down the shame first. I couldn't. Neither can you.

The rest of this chapter is some of the most important work you will ever do. I want you to treat it as such and give it the space and time it needs. Go somewhere safe. Get a journal. You can burn it later if you're worried about others reading it, but you need to write it all down. Be alone and uninterrupted. Believe in the power of living on the other side of shame enough to give yourself this space.*

I want you to name the sticky stories: the experiences; the embarrassment; the stories you never quite tell the full truth of; the things you'd rather people not know about you; the places where you feel weak and small. List them all. Maybe your list is long, maybe it's small. Maybe it extends back to elementary school, maybe it starts in college. Maybe it's work related, maybe it's sexual, maybe it's interpersonal. No one else ever has to see these words. But you have to write them down. Don't continue this chapter until you have your list.

Now, I want you to look over your list and pay attention to your body signals. Does one make your heart rate increase? Does your breathing become shallow? Does your chest tighten? Do your palms get clammy? Is there one that was the hardest to write down? Select one of your sticky stories to do this next exercise with. You might repeat it with others today or later but, for now, just choose one.

I want to take you through a visualization exercise. You're going to read it here, then go and practice it. I want you to imagine yourself talking to that younger you, the one who feels shame. The shame belongs to that earlier version of

---

* If, while doing this activity, you feel overwhelmed or unable to cope with the memories, please seek out professional help.

you, not to the you who is here today. The you who is here today has only love and forgiveness to dole out. No judgment, no shame to add. You are only a source of love.

Now, sit in a comfortable and supported position, both feet on the ground, your back supported by your seat. Close your eyes and focus on your breath. Feel the oxygen moving to every cell in your body, all the way to the tips of your fingers and the tips of your toes. Focus on the exhale. Let your exhale be three times longer than your inhale. Stay with this attention for three breaths. Now imagine that your younger self is sitting somewhere near you. Maybe in front of you, maybe beside you. Smile and share your intent to give only love. Ask them to share their shame story. Listen with compassion; no judgment, shame, or questions, only love. If you feel compelled to offer them perspective from a place of love, share it. Ask them what they are afraid of. Listen with love. If you feel compelled to reassure them from love, do so. Whatever this love compels you to do or say, do and say that. Be with this younger you as long as you need to be. If you feel like crying with them, that's ok. If you feel like comforting them while they cry, that's ok. When you feel your conversation is complete, thank them for sharing with you, send them love, and come back into this place. Before opening your eyes, come back to your breathing, wiggle your fingers, and open your eyes when you are ready.

Journal about this experience.

Now, with what you know from visiting your younger self, rewrite this story. You may need to come back to this exercise at another time. You are ready to write it when you can recognize the shame you've held in the story and it feels external to you—like you can write the story with a different moral lesson.

My Example of Shame Rewritten

In an uncomfortable and generous act of connection, I'm going to share a rewrite of my own with you.

As a consultant, I occasionally partner with other firms to deliver leadership development and strategic alignment workshops. I'd been working with a particular firm for several years as a facilitator, but I was asked to take the lead on a high-profile project. I had not been involved in the project scoping phase or early discovery conversations with the client, so I was coming in to the project with less information than I'm accustomed to, and with significant responsibility for the success of another firm's project. While we delivered what we said we would, the project did not have the impact for the client that we would expect. I carried the embarrassment and disappointment of this outcome long after the chapter was closed. When talking about it, I would build in buffers around the story to show what a bad spot I'd been in, how I had been set up to fail, and how I didn't have the partners or resources I needed to succeed. In reality, the project was a shared failure on both my part and the part of my partners. I was not a victim, just a consultant who had some things to learn.

It's ill-advised for a consultant to write into her book how she failed a client. I'm doing it anyway, because I want you to see the power that failure had over me; it clutched me in its talons and held me back from future success. In my rewritten story, I don't shy away from my errors, but neither do I paint them as indicators of future failure:

A partner organization approached me with an incredible opportunity. I was to lead a high-profile project for them with executives of a major corporation. I would have a small team and their support. The project had already been scoped out and rewarded to them, and it was my opportunity to score a win. I came into the project bold and ready. I'd led projects for this partner firm before, though never one quite as significant. Once, while the owners of the firm were out of the country on a project, I sold, created and delivered a program, on their behalf, that delighted participants and earned some of the best satisfaction ratings I'd ever achieved. I was confident in my ability to deliver quality input and facilitate needed dialogue. I had a team with me, and though we'd never worked together in the exact capacity this project required, I was sure I could lead them in a great workshop.

I had never presented the material or facilitated the work expected in this program. I had my own processes, from my firm, and believed my experience would translate to my partner firm's process easily enough. It was rather bold bravado, seeing myself as completely capable of delivering something I'd never done before, with colleagues who were not experts, a demanding and high-profile client, and someone else's process.

We delivered the material better than we should have. The participants were engaged and off their phones which, coming from executives, is akin to a five-star rating. We challenged them to think beyond their assumed boundaries, enabled them to see new synchronicities critical to their success, and accomplished more in two days than we would typically attempt. Executives personally thanked us and told us it was an incredible workshop that far exceeded their hopes and would directly impact how they did their work.

The senior executive who hired us was happy with the workshop, but afterward he asked about an output that was out of the project scope. In fact, we'd discussed this request in our pre-meeting conversations and had come to an agreement about what would and wouldn't be included. I had believed we were on the same page. I reminded him of the conversation, redirected again, and prepared for the follow-up workshop.

Though we had counseled them otherwise, the client wanted us to help them roll out their work immediately. They left no time to implement, vet or consider the change it would require of their division leaders. As the project unfolded, we realized it was largely an internal public relations activity and, as such, our process, designed to make impact and change leaders' mindsets, was the wrong fit for what was actually desired. We fulfilled our contract and, as predicted, the project fell flat. The executives who had not prepared to lead the change could not explain or defend their process and outcomes.

Ultimately, the client came back to the out-of-scope request, we gave them a costly free day to provide them with the only thing they wanted all along, which was out of the project scope and out of the firm's expertise. We got to their outcome, shook hands and parted well. I regained credibility with the owners of the partner company when they witnessed the rapport and respect the client had for me.

I learned three key lessons that have shaped every project I've led since:

1. Challenge the process and rewrite the rules to ensure you will succeed.

2. Client management is constant; do as much listening as persuading to uncover issues early.

3. Walk away from bad money, no matter how much it is. If you can't succeed for the client, it is not worth it.

If I held this as a failure story, full of my bad judgment and inability to please a client, it would prevent me from pursuing big opportunities, accepting challenging new projects and leading fellow consultants. Instead, I have rewritten it as a lesson from the school of hard knocks. I see the points where decisions led to outcomes and it has informed how I scope, what projects I take on and how I partner. Whether I, or anyone, attaches the word "failure" to this project is irrelevant to the influence it currently has on me. It has informed my process, but it did not define who I am as a consultant.

It takes courage to rewrite a shame story. It's scary, and it's one of the most powerful things you can do. Rewrite your stories. This is how you move from the power that shame holds over you, into the power of your truth. You are not that shame. It will hold you down as long as you let it. Let the retelling free you to be who you know you really are.

Now that you've reframed your stories, sorted out your mental tickertape and redefined your roles, you're able to access your inner authority and make decisions in line with who you are. You just have to discover who that is.

PART 3

DEVELOPING YOUR INNER AUTHORITY

CHAPTER 8

Discover Your Values and Your Authentic Voice

A Story of Learning to Focus on What Matters

Ryan had successfully worked his way up through his company when he became my client. His time and intellectual investment had contributed to a growth spurt there and, as an executive, he held a stake in the company and the way they were expanding. They were a private company, with a grow-and-sell strategy. Ryan stood to cash in big time in a few short years. But the pressures of his job were mounting, and he no longer bought into the stretch goals the owners were setting. He knew his team couldn't reach the targets and that they'd break their backs trying, with the lure of big bonuses. He was growing uncomfortable and was not sure he could stay. He came with many questions: What do I do? How can I possibly leave so much money on the table? I want to pursue other dreams but it seems illogical. How do I make a decision like this?

Ryan was like many of my clients: successful and being rewarded with more work. He was losing faith in his company and was unsure how to justify a decision to leave.

I remember halfway through our work together, when it was clear to me that he wanted to leave, and he knew that was the right choice for him. It took him six months to be ready to implement it and, ultimately, he found a way to leave well. When I first met him years before, he'd just left his company and asked me to read a six-page manifesto he wanted to send to his former employer. I locked gazes with him and asked, "What are you hoping to accomplish by sending this?" He likes to tell people that story with a laugh and a twinkle in his eye. He knew he tended to leave on bad terms. He didn't want that to happen this time. He knew he'd be walking away from money down the road, but he wanted to preserve as much of his investment as possible.

What Ryan had never been able to do when leaving previous jobs, was to manage his protective reactions and leave in a way that honored his values. He couldn't have said what his values were. Through our work together, he realized his value of long-term longevity was at odds with the company's growth plans. He understood that, if he stayed, this tension would remain unresolved. Similarly, he learned that he valued loyalty and did not want to burn bridges with colleagues who had invested in him. He was able to find alternative ways of remaining loyal that did not require staying with the company. By getting clear on his values and learning to recognize his defensive reactions, Ryan was able to leave the company with good grace and with relationships intact, something he had not imagined possible.

Values and the Analytical Hierarchy Process

Values drive our decision making. They cause us to weigh one choice against another in a particular way. Sometimes, a fear masks itself as a value, and gets in the way of our decision making. In Ryan's case, the fear of lost reward or lost stability tried to convince us it was equal to his values of independence, longevity, and sustainability. The fear kept him in place when his values kept nagging that he needed to go. He eventually got in line with his values and made the choice to leave.

Our values are learned. They come from our upbringing and the stories we hear in our families of origin and communities. They are both influenced by those around us and uniquely ours. When you make a tough decision, a value gets reinforced. You will choose for that value again, down the road, in part as a way of reaffirming the decision you once made. Tragedies in our lives teach us new lessons and alter our values. As we grow from our experiences, we will change how we see the world and how we interpret our values. When faced with the loss of a loved one, for example, the mourner's values about family or work-life balance might shift. While there are values that society holds in common, like honesty and fairness, your values are uniquely yours and will be interpreted by you in a way no one else can. When you discover and grow them, they become a decision-making superpower.

There's a great decision analysis tool that incorporates values, called the Analytical Hierarchy Process, often shortened to AHP, developed by Thomas L. Saaty in the 1970s. Though I'm generally skeptical of tools that claim they can help you make decisions more easily, this one does help. It doesn't do the work for you, but it does give you an easy-to-use process for acknowledging values.

First, you identify the criteria you will weigh your decision against. If you go back to my example of hiring the designer, my criteria were value, experience, style and risk mitigation.

The next and most important step is to give weight to each criterion. These factors are not all equal. Some matter more to us than others. Experience matters more to me than cost. The consideration of risk is less important than style.

Once you've set the weight of your criteria, you provide each possible choice a score out of ten, for each criterion. For example, designer one gets a five on value, an eight on experience, a nine on style and a four on risk mitigation.

This is all entered into a spreadsheet. Once you've scored each option on each criterion, the formulas do their work and out pops your answer. Based on how you weighed the criteria, and how you rated each choice on those criteria, here's what you should do.

It is important to recognize that this is not an objective tool. You choose your weight subjectively and you rate each choice subjectively. What it does is separate each criterion and give an independent score. You are not comparing designer to designer; you are comparing weighted criterion to weighted criterion. It takes the emotional guesswork and irrational thought out of the decision while leaving your values and preferences intact.

If you've ever created a pros-and-cons list and ended up choosing the "illogical" direction with too many cons or not enough pros, you've experienced the importance of weighted criteria. If every item in your list was equally important, you'd choose something with more pros than cons. But our lists are never equal.

When we are not explicit about our values, and the hierarchical weight we give to them (which might change depending on the decision at hand), we digress into internal arguments (with others and with ourselves) as to what is most important. Values give us an anchor to tie to our decision making.

They can also provide an antidote to the need for more research. I see many clients assume that they need more information if a choice is unclear. Surely, if they just gather more data, the choice will become obvious. I have never seen that work. I have rarely seen more information or more choices make the choice easier. It is most often a distraction from making the decision.

Using Your Values to Make Decisions in Practice

When my husband and I purchased our last house, ranking criteria helped immensely in getting clear on what we wanted, and what was nice to have but not critical. We laid out the features we thought we wanted in a house:

- Yard
- Sunlight
- Porch
- Four bedrooms
- Master bathroom
- Renovated kitchen
- Sunroom
- A good neighborhood
- Friendly neighbors
- Garage
- Completely updated
- Open floor plan
- Timing—moving now, not waiting

I wanted a house with a sunroom. As someone who is affected by seasonal affective disorder, moving to a state with six months of winter, I wanted a place to feel warm and bask in some sunlight. I wanted to visit every listing that had a sunroom. I was fixated on it.

My husband was fixated on a yard. We had been living on an acre lot that was severely sloped. It was not a good play space for kids under five, and it was expensive to manage—both in money and time. He favored listings with houses I would never live in, that had nice yards.

We put each of these criteria on a piece of paper and took away three, then three more, then two more, then two more until we were left with the three most important things to us collectively. They were timing, friendly neighbors, and good neighborhood. Not yard or sunroom, though those were certainly on our secondary list. The process of prioritizing criteria landed us a house we love that we probably would not have even looked at because it has neither a sunroom nor a dream yard. It does have incredible neighbors, in a neighborhood we want to be in, and it was for sale the one weekend we were in town, needing to find a place that we could buy while selling our other home. There are projects we will do on the house to get closer to some of the secondary criteria. But what is most important is that, one year later, we still agree that this was the right house for us to buy.

An important footnote to this story is that we knew how important neighborhood and neighbors were to us because we learned the hard way how much we care about those values. Our previous house was not in a neighborhood that was a match for us and, while our neighbors were friendly, the houses were far apart and we never saw each other. We learned that we don't want privacy, we want community. That was a value we hadn't realized was so important to us, until we didn't have it. It became a value we were not willing to compromise on.

And the importance of sunshine? We leased an office space downtown and a parking space ten minutes away, so I walk in the sun to and from my office every day. The yard? Our great neighbors share their space. Our kids ride their bikes up and down our neighbor's long drive for hours a day. We were still able to meet those needs in unexpected ways.

Exercise: Identifying Your Values

It's clear that knowing your values is important, but how do you discover them? Is there an assessment for that? It would be easier, wouldn't it? Unfortunately, no one else can tell you what your values are. They can reflect on how they experience you and perceive you, but that's about it. The following exercise can help you narrow down what your values are. It starts as a brainstorming exercise, then becomes a selection exercise based on heart sense. It will give you a starting point. The more attention you pay to what matters to you, the clearer you will get on your unique values.

Brainstorm answers to each of the prompts below. One answer might cause you to think of another. Write them all down. There are no wrong answers here. Your aim is to generate lots of options. Write your answers as one big list, without the questions in between.

- What values would you hope the next generation upholds?
- What values did you learn growing up?
- What is most important to you in a work culture?
- What qualities do you look for in friends?
- Why do you live where you do?
- What do you love about your job?
- If you could do any work at all, what would it be? Why?
- What do you do in your spare time? Why?
- What kind of books do you read? Why?
- What do/did you look for in a romantic partner?

Read over your entire list. Notice how you feel when you read each word. Take time to pay attention.

Make a mark next to the ten words that stand out to you as most resonant.

From these ten, circle five that are the most important to you. These are the values we are going to work with.

Draw a mind map with each of the five values as a branch. On each value draw further branches that describe what that value means for you. For example, if independence is a value, you might have the following secondary descriptor words: excellence, chosen path, decision making, freedom, and accountability. Repeat this exercise with each value.

Finally, assign a color to each value. You may close your eyes and imagine the value written. Perhaps you already see it in a particular color. When you read the question, "What color is that value?", you might immediately know. If you don't have a color association, simply assign it a color. It doesn't matter that it's "right," just that you give it a color. Color associations are an abstract yet strong connection for us. When I find a client struggling to untangle their emotional experience, talking about colors often eases the process and enables them to sort out what they are wrestling with. By assigning our values colors, we create a framework to reference in the future.

Choosing Values When the Going Gets Tough

Values are not a silver bullet. Identifying them will not make your decisions immediately easy. Here's a hard truth: knowing what your values are might make some of your decisions harder. You may look at your values and know exactly what decision will be most aligned, but you may not be ready to make that decision. Remember Ryan? It was obvious at the end of our second call that, based on values, he needed to leave his job. But he was not ready to make that decision, and it took him six months of frustration and second-guessing to get in line with his values and make the call.

The more you practice thinking about your values while making your decisions, the easier it becomes to make the hard calls. An informative exercise can be to look back on critical decisions you've made in the past and think about how they reflected your values. If you left a job, were your values at stake? What about if you left a marriage? Were your values reflected in your choice of school or major? What about where you choose to live? What makes you most annoyed or frustrated? Is it connected to your values in some way?

Many of us live our lives being influenced by our values regularly, even if we are completely unaware of it. When we begin to notice, we start to see them all around us. They shape what we buy and how we interact with our family, what sets us off and what we do when angry. As you become more aware of how they work in your life already, you'll build the muscle necessary to rely on them when decisions get hard. You might still choose not to act on your values from time to time, but you'll do it with an awareness that will enable you to be less defensive.

The Link Between Values and Authenticity

Andrea was young and in a sales role. Many of her colleagues were older men. They fit the stereotypes of salesmen: energetic, bold, willing to play hardball and tell it like it is. Andrea had stepped up her game and was vying for a promotion. To prove her capability, she was doing the job of a much higher-paid position. She was in a commission-free role, doing the work of commission earners, and reaping none of the financial rewards.

The sales guys liked Andrea, and they wanted to mentor her and give her advice. They didn't like that she was being taken advantage of, and they felt strongly that she needed to stick up for herself. They told her all the ways that they had been successful in demanding more respect.

Andrea came to me distraught about how to do this. She was angry about being taken advantage of, fired up from her most recent pep talk with the sales guys, and wanted to practice how she would march in and make some demands. The only problem was that this was not in Andrea's nature at all. She's no pushover, but she is a get-more-bees-with-honey-than-vinegar kind of person. As we talked through what mattered to her, and revisited her values, it was clear that she could not authentically have the conversation in the same way her sales friends did. She needed to confront the issue, but she needed to do it in a way that was in line with what she believed and who she wanted to be: sincere, connected and straightforward. Had she gone in with gusto, she would have been far less successful. Instead, she had a direct and heartfelt conversation with her manager, that resulted in a clear plan to achieve the promotion she sought out. It still required courage, but it didn't require false bravado. She got the promotion, and several more over the next few years. She's an up-and-comer who has survived mergers, downsizing, and restructuring. This is, in part, because she's great at what she does. It is also because she knows how to challenge in a way that is authentically aligned to her values.

Questions to Find the Authentic Choice

I'll close out this chapter with a few more questions that can help you sort out what you truly value when wavering on a decision:

- What would you do if there wasn't a wrong choice?
- What choice keeps you stuck in a role that you no longer want to play?
- What choice frees you to redefine your role?

- What kind of person gets to make this choice?

- What kind of person wouldn't make this choice?

- If you assumed everything would work out, what would you do?

- What choice gives you butterflies?

With your values and authentic voice identified, there is nothing to stop you from being a powerful decision maker. That is, unless your company isn't ready for the real you.

CHAPTER 9

Does Your Company Deserve You?

Is This a Solvable Problem?

Sometimes, even when we've done the work to manage our protective reactions, assessed if we're over-functioning or assuming something about a role we take on, learned to speak in a way that clarifies the message, sorted out our competing voices, left shame behind, and identified our values, we *still* struggle to make an empowered decision or influence others to get on board with our decisions. If you do this work and *still* struggle to make decisions in your organization, it might be them, not you.

Maybe this gives you relief. Maybe it terrifies you. If it's them, you have to leave. You will not be successful in an organization with competing values. You know too much about who you are to check at the door all of those things that matter to you. If you were struggling to be successful, now you know why. Sometimes you cannot be successful playing their game. The great news is that there are other games. The bad news is that you have to find them.

This chapter is going to focus on how to assess if there are more inherent issues that will always keep you down in your current company. It does not mean the company is bad. You might really like the company, and you might love the people you get to work with, or the work you get to do. But you picked up this book because you wanted something to change and, if there is a cultural mismatch, you will not be successful there. If it still isn't working, it's not you, it's them.

Earlier, I told you that your highest brain functions shut down in emotional stress. If you're mastering your defensive reactions, sorting out the voices and releasing shame and you still feel that emotional stress, there is something else amiss. Let's explore that.

Organizations have cultures. Often, they also have principles or values that they tout as important for company and employee success. But naming values doesn't always name the culture. Sometimes a company defines a value or principle differently than an employee might. Here are some common mismatches I see between organizations and employees. These are signs of cultural incompatibility:

1. Collaborative environment: The organization expects lots and lots of buy-in, while you value autonomy and a team that trusts your decisions. The organization might make decisions via a committee, as a way to break down

silos. It probably slows down decisions. If you like to make fast decisions and move, this could drive you nuts, and you may not have the skills necessary (and may have little interest in developing them) to succeed in this environment.

2. Innovation: The company expects careful and strategic innovation, whereas you want to experiment and fail fast. Some companies want new ideas, but they want them carefully tested. If you come with a fast trial-and-error, test-and-fail approach, you will quickly become frustrated.

3. Teamwork: The company values politeness and they believe speaking kindly and carefully builds trust in teams. You want to hold people accountable and improve. Teamwork can mean keeping the peace and making nice, or it can mean rumble, challenge and improve. A "rumbler" will ruffle a lot of feathers in a peacekeeping environment.

4. Performance: The company wants to maintain its current success, whereas you want to push for growth. Some companies are comfortable with the status quo. They talk about performance as something that sustains existing customer relationships. If performance to you means growth and outperforming the competition, you might feel frustrated in an environment that doesn't feel the urgency you do. You might see mediocrity all around you, and your efforts to improve are met with rejection.

5. Growth: The company is committed to growing by whatever means, whereas you believe growth should happen carefully and sustainably. Though you might both want to see the company grow, they might be willing to test the company's limits and you might see that as an unwise risk that will cost the company talent. You will inevitably end up in a tug-of-war and you are likely to lose.

6. Care for people: The company believes that showing care means rewarding employees for hard work, whereas you see care as protection from overwork. If the company expects long hours, they might still tout care for people as a value, and define that by rewarding them with bonuses. If, to you, care means respecting the work-life balance and not overburdening people, you will feel misaligned.

7. Respect: The company expects employees to respect authority, while you expect everyone to respect humanity. You both tout respect as a core value. In the company, it means respecting hierarchy and not rocking the boat. To you, it means inherently respecting people and their different ideas and beliefs. You want to be respected when you share an opinion, and they shut you down.

8. Independence: The company expects you to define your role and success, but you want to be given the parameters and expectations to work within. They say it's a job that requires independent thinking because they don't

know what is needed, and they want an expert to work it out and show them. You want independence in how you do your work, but you expect feedback on what is required. They are frustrated that you keep asking questions that they can't answer. You are frustrated because you don't have any metrics for success to guide you.

It becomes apparent that there are so many ways for an organization and individual to use the same language to mean vastly different things.

Identifying the Values Gap Between You and Your Company

I was once working with the executives of a division, in one of the largest US-based global companies. We were identifying the leadership behaviors that would be necessary for them to achieve their strategic goals. Agreeing to the behaviors wasn't hard. An important behavior to the team was trust. It was when we asked them to define trust that conflict occurred. The head of the division believed that a drive for results would bring about trust. If they focused singularly on getting results, they would be able to build trust to make decisions together. A leader from Europe scoffed, "You expect to get results without trusting me first?" After discussion and probing, what he was saying was, "How can I trust you to not take advantage of me?" A value clash over the same words was emerging. The European leader defined trust as core to building relationships, something to be assumed and fostered. The American division head defined trust as something earned for excellent results, and potentially withheld.

Now, this does not mean the European leader could not be successful in the company. The two leaders were hashing out the culture they wanted to build for their division. The discussion was critical to getting it right and getting everyone on board. You do not want an organization full of homogenous robots, who all think the same thing, in the same way. But neither do you want people who cannot get on board with the company's culture.

When leaders are given feedback about their work, it's generally positioned as a performance gap. You are doing A, and you need to be doing B. Here's a plan to move you to B. Sometimes, these are skills gaps, and putting the right work in gets you to B. But sometimes, these are values gaps and seeking to close them will be difficult and sometimes harmful to the person. Many organizations want their leaders to succeed because it is costly to replace talent. If they see one of these gaps in a leader they want to keep, they will invest in that leader's development to close the gap. This is always done for the organization's benefit, sometimes with benefit to the employee. But if the gap is a values gap, meaning a conflict of values where the organization's expectations conflict with your values, the development plan can become harmful.

Take emotional intelligence as an example. Daniel Goleman, the author who popularized the now-common concept, describes it as the ability to recognize, understand and manage our emotions and recognize, understand and influence the emotions of others. These are valuable skills, and they are associated with leaders at the highest levels of nearly all major international companies. It is a skill to be adept at emotional regulation. It is also valuable to be skillful at adapting yourself to best influence others. But how do you ensure that you adapt in a way that honors your values? How would you know if you can successfully demonstrate emotional intelligence while still maintaining your differentiated values, or if the insistence on your development has more to do with fitting in and not rocking the boat?

Is it an Intent-Impact Gap or a Behavior-Values Gap?

Adapting your style to better speak another's language, if you will, will make you a more successful influencer. It might also ask you to silence your own values, just a bit, to be able to better relate to another person. However, it takes a very advanced and developed person to do this well. Only about one percent of the US population is that developed, according to the adult developmental theory laid out by Robert Kegan.[17]

Kegan asserts that there are five stages of development:

- **Stage 1:** The Impulsive Mind (Found in young children)
- **Stage 2:** The Imperial Mind (Mostly adolescence; six percent of the adult population never advances beyond this stage)
- **Stage 3:** The Socialized Mind (Fifty-eight percent of adults are here. This stage focuses on fitting into society and conforming)
- **Sage 4:** The Self-Authoring Mind (This is thirty-five percent of adults and where you start to understand and make decisions based on individual, rather than collective, values)
- **Stage 5:** The Self-Transforming Mind (One percent of the adult population is here. At this stage, individuals can embrace paradox. From this stage, you can effectively adapt to the values of others, without losing your own value identity)

Pay attention when your company asks you to develop emotional intelligence. Although it is a critical component of Stage 5, the Self-Transforming Mind, it can sometimes be misused as a tool to knock leaders back into Stage 3, the Socialized Mind. Remember that only about one percent of the adult population makes it past a Self-Authoring Mind. Is your organization actually saying, "Learn to adapt yourself so you can fit in and be like the rest of us. Stop rocking the boat. Your inability to code-switch and be like us means you don't have emotional intelligence." Unfortunately, emotional intelligence is sometimes a weapon in organizations used to homogenize.

When I coach leaders, I generally insist on conducting a 360; a set of interview or survey questions asked of the leader's direct reports, peers, and manager(s). The information I gather does two things: it helps me understand the perception of my client within the organization, and it helps me recognize misalignment between what the organization expects and who the client is willing and able to be. Often, the gap is not about values. It may be about the unintended impacts of a leader's behavior. We all have blind spots, where our intent doesn't align with our impact. For example, we may intend to hold someone accountable for a mistake in a meeting so the team can learn from their mistakes and grow. The impact, in reality, is that an employee feels belittled and embarrassed in front of their peers. Recognizing and managing blind spots like this is critical work for leaders to reconcile their intent and impacts. For a leader to grow their influence in an organization, they must know and manage the perceptions of their leadership style. Ideally, perception, impact, and intent all align.

However, sometimes I don't see intent-impact gaps, but rather behavior-values gaps. What I mean by this is that I might learn that the executives believe Joe is arrogant. What I've learned from Joe, in our values conversations, is that he is a debater and a quick thinker, with a passion for excellence. He wants a team to debate many sides of an idea, believing that rigorous discussion will bring out the best solutions, and make everyone better. He doesn't care if the ultimate idea is his, but he will argue for his idea until he feels it gets a fair shake. I could work with Joe to manage the perception that he is arrogant. But it will be very hard to do this without dampening Joe's value of debate and excellence. We need to explore whether he is a cultural misfit because there is a gap between the desired behavior and Joe's values. Joe may not be able to close that gap without compromising his values.

When I chose to leave my corporate job, I knew that I was in a behavior-values gap, not an intent-impact gap. When I was hired, I was in a creative department with people who challenged each other, and tested boundaries and celebrated wins together. After a reorganization, the development arm was under a department that valued process, predictability, and conservatism. My values would never align in this new context and I would not succeed. I tried growing smaller to bridge the gap, and it only succeeded in making me miserable. The risk of staying was greater than the risk of leaving. I might have been able to be successful in another part of the organization but, as a niche leadership development person, there were no other roles. My only option was to leave. It was scary and it felt like a failure. However, from my current vantage point, it was a raging success.

I learned what mattered to me and I took a stand for it. I walked away from something that was diminishing me and any future impact I might have. I did the work of shedding shame and fear of failure. I created something wildly successful and wildly meaningful.

Are you in an intent-impact gap? Or a behavior-values gap? Consider the assessment below. It will not answer your question, but it should give you insight.

Exercise: Assessing the Value Gap

List your values in a table like the one below. On a scale of one (low) to ten (high), rate how supportive your work environment is of you acting on that value in the "Enactment" column. For example, if your value, from your mind map, is independence (excellence, chosen path, decision making, freedom, accountability), how supported do you feel to make decisions that bring that value to life? Next, rate how often that value is pursued in your department. Finally, rate how often that value is pursued in your company.

Value	Enactment	Department	Company
Independence	5	7	2

Explore the data you see here. In the "Enactment" column, pay attention to scores between five and seven. This could explain some of your discomfort with your company. These scores don't represent misalignment, but they can represent discomfort. Do you have any scores below five? That is likely a misalignment that cannot be fixed.

When I did this exercise for the corporate job where I was a misfit, the numbers were astonishing. Two of my values I was originally able to enact at an eight, but they moved to a two after the restructure! And the highest the department received, for any of my values, was a two. Several of them were a zero. When looking at the department before the restructure, my alignment was much stronger. I simply could not be successful in the new environment, in any way that was authentic to me.

If your values seem to be in a zone you're willing to accept, then consider the gaps you have been told you need to improve on. If you've been given any feedback about your impact that you think is out of alignment with your intent, make note of it. Across from each gap, identify the corporate cultural element being expressed. For example, if you've been told others think you're arrogant, you would write arrogant on the left. Across from it, you would identify the corporate culture being expected—perhaps teamwork, politeness, or humility. Try to stay neutral or positive in your language. The company is not bad for having this culture, even if it goes against your value. Examples of negative responses would be keeping peace, complacency, and mediocrity. No company values those things, and it is rife with judgment. For this exercise to be beneficial, you need to be as objective and judgment-free as possible.

Examine the cultural elements you identified. Look back at your values. Are there any clashes? Do you have personal values that work against the cultural elements you identified? If you answered yes, you might have a behavior-value gap, and your attempts to close them will not be in your best interests. The perception of arrogance might be treated as a desire for quality in a different organization with different cultural norms.

Gap	Organizational Value	Value Conflict?
Arrogance	Teamwork and Humility	Perhaps—I value straightforward debate

Should I Stay or Go?

By now, you probably have either a gut sense or a heart sense for that answer. Generally, I find that if my clients are asking the question, they know that the answer is that they should go, but they aren't quite ready to commit to an exit plan. You should know the risk of staying by now. It might be your sense of growth, your career progression, or your fulfillment. And, for many of my clients, there are very sound reasons why they are willing to risk those things. I support their decisions when they are active choices. And, like Ryan, when they decide they are finally ready to move on and want to do it well, I support them in those actions.

Only you know the risks you will take by leaving. Family, location, salary, and security all come in to play when wrestling with a decision of this magnitude. You now have tools to help reconcile this:

- Getting clear on roles: Will your company renegotiate your role with you so it aligns with your values and skills more appropriately?

- Tough conversations: Address problems head-on and use these tools to have real conversations, at home and work. There may be solutions that you haven't thought of.

- Know when you're being defensive: If you live in a defensive state, moving on will not solve this. Other organizations might ruffle your feathers less, but this will haunt you in other places as well. Work on minimizing this as a variable.

- Know which voice is telling you to go, and which is telling you to stay: Hold a board meeting with your inner voices and consider them from a place of love and neutrality.

- Can you leave the shame you've assumed in this organization? Will it let you? If not, you must move on.

- Finally, can you live your values here, or will they be compromised?

All of these decision-making factors come down to you making the biggest decision before you. Is your work environment keeping you from being the kind of decision maker you're capable of becoming? In the right environment, with the tools in this book under your belt, anyone can change the authenticity and confidence with which they make decisions.

Years ago, I was gifted a piece of art that remains one of the most meaningful reminders of choosing to step away from irreconcilable gaps. It's a beautiful mixed media piece, including a quote from Kobi Yamada that reads, "Sometimes you just have to take the leap and build your wings on the way down." And, so it is. Next, we'll explore how to best support that flight.

CHAPTER 10

How to Stay on Track

Putting Learning into Practice

When I first became a leadership development practitioner, a friend told me the story of his boss who loved personal development. This boss had a series of tapes (it was the '80s) that he would listen to every day. There were tapes on being a better manager and mentor. There were tapes on communication. Tapes on influencing. He liked to talk about his tapes. He valued learning and growth, and wanted to share that value with others; he expected that his commitment to his tapes would inspire his team. In my friend's opinion, he managed the team the same way in 1980 as he did in 2000. Though he believed that study would make him better, he never integrated the learning in any perceivable way for his team.

It's a tragedy and, unfortunately, it's quite common. For development to happen, you can't stop at learning. You must also implement and measure the impact. Learning and development teams in corporations throughout the world have sought to measure their effectiveness and prove impact as a way of defending their legitimacy. The work of Donald Kirkpatrick lays out four levels of measurement in relation to evaluating learning[18]:

1. **Level 1:** Did they like it?
2. **Level 2:** Did they learn it intellectually (Often measured with a quiz. Notice how we still use school-age learning techniques here?)
3. **Level 3:** Have they put it into practice i.e. has it changed behavior?
4. **Level 4:** Is the change in behavior impacting results?

My friend's boss mastered Level 1, and probably Level 2, but he stopped there. He never put it into practice, so no one around him saw results. As nice as those tapes might have been, all they did was create a false level of confidence in his ability to manage his team well.

How do you avoid that trap? Well, you've made it to Chapter Ten. You've hopefully even paused to do the exercises, reflect on your obstacles to flow, and consider the tools that will help you gain buy-in and speak from a place of inner authority. What will it take for this to become more than an increase in your fund of knowledge? How will you practice these tools, especially when they feel awkward? And, I promise you, the first few times out of the gate, they will feel awkward.

The Change Curve Holds You Back

The change management industry has shown us that we are more comfortable doing something that we know is not correct, but that we can do well, than we are doing the right thing poorly. In our ever-evolving growth and development, we strive to get better at things. We want to do things well. We've been rewarded for this our entire life. When change happens to us, we need to learn to do a new thing and, at the outset, we are generally quite bad at it. Consider the following examples:

- New parents learning to care for a newborn.
- Starting a job in a new industry, and learning about an unfamiliar context.
- Shifting from being a team leader to a divisional leader.
- Learning to play an instrument.

Most of us have developed a fixed mindset, not a growth mindset. We say, "I can't do that" rather than, "I'm not good at it yet." In our youngest educational years, we were not expected to be experts; we were expected to be learners. Yet, when we graduated from our last level of education, most of us shifted our mindset to believe we were "set" and shut off our growth mindset. Our jobs often reinforce this by rewarding competency. This isn't a bad thing—we should reward good work—but it can hardwire us into a fixed mindset. We are trained to want to prove our mastery of a skill in return for the reward, when what's needed for long-term success is a growth mindset willing to learn new skills and adapt to new contexts.

A pitfall that many newly-promoted leaders fall into is assuming that, because they are now in an authority role, they need to have mastered the content of the team they are leading when, in actuality, their growth is in letting others be experts.

I worked with an executive in a financial institution that prides itself on moving people around and building breadth of exposure to new skills. This leader had recently been promoted to lead a multifunctional team of deep-knowledge experts. He had only perfunctory knowledge of their work. He was distraught and experiencing significant stress at the thought of learning the work of so many different experts in order to be able to lead the team and give them advice. Up until now he was successful because he was the expert. But that wasn't his role now (think back to Chapter Five on redefining roles). His role was to be the strategic leader, connected with other divisions, and relaying strategic direction down to his departments. He needed to trust the expertise of his team.

This executive needed to practice managing people without understanding their work in depth. He needed to be able to say "I don't know your work as well as you, but I'll help you think through it," rather than, "This is what we need to do." It was awkward and he worried he would lose their respect. He was more comfortable assuming he should learn everything about every function he now oversaw, as unrealistic as he knew that to be. He had to flex his growth mindset in order to trust he could learn a new way of managing.

We need to be willing to do a new thing awkwardly. We must try it, learn from the experience, adapt, and try again, if we have any hope of learning to do something new. As inconvenient as it is, we cannot move from doing the wrong thing well, to doing the right thing well, without spending some time in the messy space of doing the right thing poorly. This is where many people stop. They might dip their toe into that growth place but find it uncomfortable and inadvertently, often unconsciously, choose to stay in the comfortable place of doing the wrong thing well.

Stop Saying You Just Can't Change

In their book, *Immunity to Change*[19], Robert Kegan and Lisa Laskow Lahey explore what keeps people doing the wrong thing even when it goes against their own stated goals. We have competing priorities, often unconsciously. The best example is a resolution to get in shape. Most people state this goal at least once in their lives, many really believe that they are ready to commit to it, and yet most people can't maintain the momentum and fall back into their old habits. What happens? Why can't a fully functioning adult, one who manages and achieves many goals in their work, follow through on a commitment to getting in shape? It's because they are more committed to something else that conflicts with getting in shape.

Maybe they are concerned about being associated with the stereotype of inconsistent, yoyo dieters. When eating out with friends, they don't make healthy choices because they want to maintain a care-free, not-body-conscious image. They could be pressed for sleep, and find that their expected routine of waking up early to exercise competes with their higher priority of being well-rested. Perhaps they value time with their kids after school, and a post-work gym session would take away family time that is more important to them. The kicker in all of this is that they still value and want to commit to getting in shape, but there are other priorities getting in their way. Until they name and resolve these competing priorities, they will never meet their goal of getting in shape.

Add to all of this the adult development stages we learned about in Chapter Nine. Even if you've embraced a growth mindset and overcome your competing priorities, there may be people in your life who want you to keep doing the old thing, even if it's no longer "right" for you. They may have opinions about you, and your belief that "right" now looks different. A group of people functioning in a socialized developmental stage (as explained in Chapter Nine) will try to pull you back to their way of doing things.

So, not only do you have to go through the discomfort of doing the right thing poorly, but you also have to do it while being criticized by others who don't understand the growth you seek. This is why so many people stay stuck and never move past listening to the tapes.

The good news is that you can move through all of these challenges, and come out the other side, becoming the great decision maker you know you are capable of being. To master this, you will need help. You will need accountability, support, encouragement, challenge, and belief from another person. You will need someone else to hold the vision with you as you live in the discomfort of doing the right thing poorly.

The Challenges with Growth

Here are the challenges I see my clients face, and what can happen when they fall back into their old patterns:

- The people around them question their growth; maybe not their ability but the validity in what they are doing. These people may not understand who you are trying to become and would like to keep you predictable. The client gets sucked back into the roles they tried to redefine, and ends up complying with the pressure for the status quo. They finally accept their identity as being unable to make tough calls, and get used to the idea of this being the most they'll ever do professionally.

- Their protective systems kick into gear at the discomfort of trying new things. Without support, and the challenge to push through, they heed these warnings and go back to the safety of repeating old patterns and doing what is familiar.

- The inner critic pops up, uninvited and often unrecognized, and they don't have the skill to name it, understand it and help it step aside. They believe the inner critic's messages that they "can't do it", or that their expectations are too high, and they shrink back down to a size that the inner critic feels is safer.

- The old stories of past failures and disappointments pop back up, and they start believing them to be harbingers of what's to come. Without someone challenging them to change their perspective, they remain rooted in the shame of their past.

- They don't explore the full depth of their values. The first time they are faced with someone who holds a different set of values, they accept these and theirs get put in a drawer rather than used as a tool for developing their inner authority.

- The fear of the unknown impact of a career or company change becomes louder than the knowledge that they are in the wrong place. They stay committed to an organization that will keep them down, rather than finding the job and company that aligns with who they are.

You will always do more, and faster, with a trainer at a gym than you will on your own. They are the experts on your growth, and they know how to push you further and convince you to do more. You will not run as fast, lift as much, or do the extra rep without them. It's the same with personal development. It's not impossible, but it's harder, takes longer and requires incredible discipline.

I challenge my clients to move beyond a Level 2 understanding of this work, and push them to put it into practice and find results. I help them jump off the cliff, knowing that the parachute will open. Clients who see the process through find amazing outcomes.

This work isn't for everyone. It is not for people who see others as the problem and want them to change. It is not for people who like mental exercise but aren't ready to be challenged. And it is not for people who are perfectly comfortable with where they are. It will grow you into a stronger, more capable, more confident decision maker, and to do that requires your commitment to rise to the challenge.

If you don't want to stay in this role forever; if you don't want this to be all there is; if you don't want to go back-and-forth on decisions and mistrust your intuition; and if you're ready to *do the work*, then working with me will change your life.

You're ready to form a plan to make this dream a reality.

CHAPTER 11

What to Do Now

Becoming the Decision Maker Extraordinaire

When Shante began her coaching with me, neither of us could have predicted the person she'd become as a result. She'd shed her anger and stopped making herself small enough to fit into other people's expectations. She'd learned to manage her protective reactions and speak the truth in a way that brought others in, rather than distancing them. Our work was "just" supposed to be about becoming a better leader, but she'd changed the way she saw herself and the world around her. It was remarkable, powerful, inspiring. She even stood taller.

This framework doesn't just make you a better decision maker, it develops you into an authentic leader. The truth is that you cannot be a better decision maker without developing your inner authority. The authentic leader knows what matters and isn't afraid to stand up for it. They can both listen to other perspectives and retain their integrity by holding on to what they know to be true. They can gain new perspectives on their roles and assumptions, and seek out the right conversations to renegotiate them when they no longer fit. The authentic leader, with inner authority, knows the rules and gets to choose which ones to respect and which to step around.

I've written a lot from the perspective of a coach, sharing my clients' stories in the hopes of inspiring your growth. I'm also a mother of two young boys. It has been my role as a parent that has shaped me the most to write this book. I didn't know how firm the walls were on the boxes we put kids inside, until my children tried to break down those walls. I've been surprised to learn how narrowly we define boyhood and masculinity, even at the earliest ages. Having experienced it firsthand, I was already quite aware of the boxes we put girls in. Boxes like these can squash our inner authority and our ability to be an authentic leader.

As I help my clients redefine their worlds and stand in line with their inner authority, I hope to help create a world that is a little more accepting of all of aspects of our children. They will eventually become the adults that build the future. As cliché as it is to write that, it is what drives the work I do—to unleash the adults who have functioned inside boxes they've outgrown, and to make space for the kids who don't yet know the boundaries of boxes.

An Overview of the Process
and Its Impacts

The tools in this book change lives. Even if you've done none of the exercises (which I hope isn't the case), you are now broadly thinking about decision making. It is no longer (only) about using these tools and processes to weed out your biases and make a "rational" decision, it is now about who you are as the decision maker.

I laid out the harsh reality that your best-made decisions will get overlooked if you can't influence and bring others into your process. By learning to listen and connect with the people around you, by loosening the reins on being the *one who knows*, you can empower others to make decisions, listen in a way that builds their trust, and advocate for your ideas from a place of compassion, connection and influence.

I taught the impact that the amygdala and defensive system can have on how you react to others and make decisions in difficult situations, and gave you tools for calming the warning signals it sends out. By enlisting the help of meditation exercises and centering tools, I showed you how to ground yourself in the power of presence and override the signals telling you to clam up, rage or walk away.

I gave you permission to examine the roles you play, both those that are real and those you've invented. I challenged you to choose what to accept, what to reject and what to tweak. When you challenge your assumptions, you will be better able to accommodate the stressors that come with any role. When you accept only the roles you believe in, the pressure feels more manageable.

I gave you exercises for listening to and talking with the many contradictory voices that pass through your thoughts. I taught you to stop trying to "overcome" them, and to instead hear their concerns in a way that allows them to step back. Once you've given them a voice, you can move forward with what you know to be true.

I urged you to see your shame for what it is: an old story holding you back. I taught you to wrestle with these shameful past tales that were keeping you on high alert in order to avoid making the same mistake twice. I pushed you to reassess the reality of the experience, and rewrite the moral of the story, so you could strip away its power over you.

I helped you to find your values—the ones that drive who you are and why you do what you do. When you work through the tools designed to help you listen to and employ your values, they will become your special weapons when you feel like you're in a decision-making fog.

I asked you to truly engage with the question, "Should I stay or should I go?" By analyzing your company's cultural expectations against your own values, you can decide if that company can support an authentic you, or if you are out of alignment and would thrive (not just survive) somewhere else.

Exercise: Defining Positive Changes and Making a 'To-Be' List

There is one more exercise. I want you to examine what will need to change for you to be the person you've discovered in this book. Rather than brainstorming a list of roadblocks and barriers, and quickly getting into a this-will-never-work mental model, I want you to identify positive changes—things you can add, create, repurpose—toward this new you.

For example, you might identify the following:

- Change how I talk with Tina by listening more and drawing her into decisions.

- Set aside 15 minutes a day to journal and don't go home until it's complete.

- Set an intention before I exercise and exercise every weekday.

- Talk with my wife about how we manage money.

- Use my rewritten story in my next town hall meeting.

Prioritize three to five to-dos that you will start with. When you accomplish those, select three to five more. Do not try to tackle everything at once. It's not possible and your efforts will be diffuse. Choose a few meaningful things to start with and go from there.

Now that you have your "to-do" list, you need to create a "to-be" list. We are so good at making "to-do" lists because we relish crossing things off of them! But now I want you to reflect on all that you've discovered about yourself in this book. I want you to consider who you now need to *be* to make authentic decisions.

Consider your reclaimed roles, the listener-in-you, the reframed stories, your values, and let yourself imagine who this person is. Who do you need to be to put this person into the world?

Close your eyes, feel the ground beneath your feet, focus on your breath, and imagine yourself as the decision maker you could be. Picture yourself in a board room, or around your dining room table, or in a team huddle, showing up as completely you, completely authentic. What are you saying? How do you appear to others? What is your tone? How does it feel? After several minutes watching yourself, open your eyes and spend five minutes writing about that experience. After your writing reflection, answer the question: who do I need to be to make decisions like I know I can?

Wise People Make Time to Reflect

Reflection is not something we make much time for. We're so busy making and crossing items off lists that sitting and thinking seems wasteful. It is not. It is one of the most productive things you can do. You've learned several writing prompts and journaling tricks throughout this book. Come back to them. You will need time to process your learning and reflect on your successes and failures. If you assume you will grow without reflection, you are likely to slip back into the status quo!

Carve out time in your schedule for reflection. I do it daily, 15 minutes every morning. You might find it more beneficial at the end of the workday, or before going to bed. Research suggests that the act of writing with a pen creates more brain synapses than typing.[20] Trust that research, get off your technology, and write in a book.

Find Grace for the People Around You

A final note on growth and development as a professional with colleagues, friends, and family: not everyone is growing at the same rate. Some of the people in your life are stuck. They have not read this book and they may not be ready to. Some of them are just plain disinterested in moving past their socialized mind. When we commit to this work, it feels *so good* that we want it for all of the people we care about. It can be bewildering and even painful if they reject it.

The best advice I've ever been given came after an intense workshop week that gave me growth in a way I was hardly prepared for. It was magical and empowering and enlightening and I was ready to be a whole new me in the world. The facilitators wisely encouraged us at the end of the workshop to "be gracious with the people in your life who have not benefited from this workshop."

Wow. That meant being gracious in light of their ignorance. Be gracious when they don't understand what I'm saying. Be gracious when they act out defensively. Be gracious when they hold on tightly to old behaviors. Offer grace.

As you renegotiate your roles, old stories, and beliefs, you find freedom and, in doing that, you enable others to find freedom too, in their own time and their own way. Popularized when misattributed to Nelson Mandela's 1994 Inaugural address, author Marianne Williamson's now famous quote states "As we let our own light shine, we unconsciously give other people permission to do the same. As we are liberated from our own fear, our presence automatically liberates others."

Thank you for allowing me to be your guide to finding your decision flow.

ACKNOWLEDGEMENTS

This book would not be possible without so many people offering support, encouragement, and ideas during the process. My husband, Andrew Lessard, has been a stalwart champion of my work. Not just as my number one cheerleader, but also as my business partner. His patience, encouragement, belief, and presence got me through this process. I'm so grateful for his willingness to fill in the cracks while I devoted myself to this work.

To the OBs from our Coachella retreat—you were the first spark that made this happen. Though I hadn't yet dreamed this up, your light lit something in me that turned into a whole new way of thinking. Kathryn Hall, your love and life have been by my side on this entire coaching journey. Alene Gabriel, you challenge and laugh in ways that make me uncomfortable and shake things loose. Meg Buzzi, you worked magic on me in ways you'll never know during our side conversations. Erin Fitzsimmons, I just knew you were supposed to be in my life from that first car ride and there's no turning back now! Staci, EB, and Jenn, your presence and spirits lifted me and landed me here. Thank you all!

A very special thank you goes to David Lapin and Desi Rosenfield of Lapin International. You saw something in me I didn't yet see, nurtured it, and gave me space to experiment. Thank you for trusting me and opening so many doors. David, your wisdom and push for excellence has changed how I think. Desi, you've been an incredible mentor to me and an inspiring teacher. To my other colleagues at Lapin—your light and commitment to the client are an inspiration and together we do amazing things! Michael Forlenza, you've been an incredible partner over the years. I've learned from you, and with you, and you've helped to shape this work. Thank you.

And, goodness, to all my clients who have trusted me with their stresses, concerns, and, of course, their successes! This book is an homage to your work. I learned from you how to do this. Thank you for bravely stepping into self-reflection, the willingness to challenge your ideas, and the courage to grow into something bigger. I have a deep respect for every one of you.

A special thank you to Angela Lauria, and the staff of The Author Incubator. You helped me realize I already was the person who could write this book. My developmental editor, Ora North, and my managing editor, Bethany Davis, helped me find the story in this book.

Sarah Busby, your editing helped turn this book into magic. Thank you for your excitement for this book and for pushing me to make it so much better.

ABOUT THE AUTHOR

Erin Clymer Lessard is a decision-making expert who has coached and consulted leaders in Fortune 500 firms around the world. After working internally as an organizational consultant in the financial services industry, Erin founded Lessard Consulting to help companies build better teams and develop their leaders. She has coached clients on three continents, consulted in some of the US's largest multinationals, and loves bringing that expertise to nonprofits and small- and medium-sized companies.

Erin's approach is influenced by her studies in organizational systems and psychological and social adult development. She blends a results-oriented drive and reflective practice to transform hundreds of clients' lives.

Erin is a professional certified coach (PCC, International Coaching Federation), a certified professional co-active coach (CPCC), and a certified coach and facilitator for Lead by Greatness, StrengthsFinder and DiSC. Erin holds an MBA from Duquesne University.

Erin loves the outdoors and can often be found enjoying all of the seasons where she lives and plays in southern Maine.

THANK YOU

Thank you for reading *Decision Flow*. Going through this process has the potential to change your life, like it has for hundreds of my clients. I always hate it when a good book ends, so I want to offer you a special gift. Access an exclusive 30-minute online class, designed especially for readers of this book: www.lessardconsulting.com/decision-making-class

I want to keep you moving toward being the kind of person who can make authentic decisions in flow! Take advantage of this resource and keep your momentum going.

ENDNOTES

1. Csikszentmihalyi, M. *Flow: The Psychology of Optimal Experience,* Harper and Row, 1990.

2. Scharmer, O. "Uncovering the Blind Spot of Leadership," Thedailygood.com, July 9, 2013.

3. Lammers, J., Stoker, J., Rink, F., & Galinsky, A. "To Have Control Over or to be Free from Others? The Desire for Power Reflects a Need for Autonomy," Society for Personality and Social Psychology, March, 2016.

4. Vohn, K. D., Baumeister, R. F., Twenge. J. M., Schmeichel, B. J., & Tice, D. M. "Decision Fatigue Exhausts Self-Regulatory Resources," Psychology Today, n.d.

5. Lencioni, P. *Five Dysfunctions of a Team,* Jossey-Bass, 2002.

6. Patterson, G., & McMillan, S. *Crucial Conversations,* McGraw Hill, 2012.

7. Adapted from the Ladder of Inference by Peter Senge in *The Fifth Discipline: The Art and Practice of the Learning Organization,* Doubleday, 2006.

8. Goleman, D. *Emotional Intelligence: Why it can Matter More than IQ,* Bantam, 2005.

9. Kahneman, D. *Thinking Fast and Slow,* Farrar, Straus and Giroux, 2011

10. Ireland, T. "What Does Mindfulness Do to Your Brain," Scientific American, June 2014.

11. Porges, S. *The Polyvagal Theory: Neurophysiologial Foundations of Emotions, Attachment, Communication and Self-Regulation,* W.W. Norton & Company, 2001.

12. Bolte, A., Goschke, T., & Kulh, J. "Emotion and Intuition: Effects of Positive and Negative Mood on Implicit Judgements of Semantic Coherence," *Psychological Science,* 2003.

13. Johnson, B. *Polarity Management,* HRD Press, 1996.

14. Schwartz, R. *Introduction to the Internal Family Systems Model,* Trailheads Publications, 2001.

15. Brown, B. *Dare to Lead: Brave Work. Tough Conversations. Whole Hearts,* Random House, 2018.

16. Hasher, L., Goldstein, D., & Toppino, T. "Frequency and the Conference of Referential Validity," *Journal of Verbal Learning and Verbal Behavior.* Academic Press, September 2005.

17. Kegan, R., & Laskow, L. *Immunity to Change: How to Overcome it and Unlock the Potential in Yourself and Your Organization,* Harvard Business Review Press, 2009.

18. Kirkpatrick, J., & Kayser, W. *Kirkpatrick's Four Levels of Training Evaluation,* Association for Talent Development, 2016.

19. Ibid.

20. Study referenced in: Doubek, J. "Attention, Students: Put Your Laptops Away," NPR, 2016.

www.ingramcontent.com/pod-product-compliance
Lightning Source LLC
Chambersburg PA
CBHW050506210326
41521CB00011B/2345